Authored and Photographed by Wong How Man

NATURE IN MY MIND

自然所想

黃效文 著

序

好奇心和良知驅使 HM 前進到千年來情勢緊繃的地方。
透過他攝影家的眼睛，我們看到了他在世界角落所看
到的，和正在發生的改變；透過他探索新聞的觸角，
我們也跟著他發掘那些萌芽或消失中的問題。他將我
們這些讀者帶進他的探險世界，我不禁好奇，我們這
些人到底有沒有像他那樣的洞察力和體力與冰雪中最
後一位馴鹿牧人交心、復育純種的緬甸貓、定位依洛
瓦底江的源頭、紀錄消失中的巴塔克族。而近期 HM
更拓展他的目光遠到義大利的製琴師，提醒我們改變
不僅在自然界裡發生。

HM 從不斷論。他觀察，學習。他教導──他希望可以
影響下個世代，讓他們有條不紊地探索、記錄事實，
讓更多的讀者，像我們這樣坐在沙發裡的觀察者，也
可以察覺到他的發現。

FOREWORD

Curiosity and conscience drive Wong How Man. Immersed in the tension between places as they were for many millennia and the stark change he sees emerging, How Man uses his photographer's eye to share his recognition of the impact of the incursion of the outside world. His journalistic probing uncovers nascent issues. We, as viewers and readers, revel in his ventures and adventures wondering if we could have the insight and strength to herd reindeer in Siberia or revive the Burmese cat as a pure line or be a watchman over the source of the Irrawaddy or the chronicler of the disappearance of the Batak. In recent travels, How Man has widened his search to man-made phenomena such as the luthiers of Italy to remind us that all change in not found in nature.

How Man never judges. He observes and learns. He teaches — hoping that he will infect the next generation with the desire to explore methodically and record the facts so that a wider audience, those of us who are armchair observers, may become aware.

HM 所做的事激發我自己對亞洲的興趣。他告訴我過去與現在發生的故事。他讓我了解巨大的改變正在亞洲各地進行，不只是在經濟上、政治上，社群、人們、自然也同時在改變。他鮮明的描述讓我發覺原來亞洲存在著這些景象。HM 的這些故事和紀錄將會隨著時間而顯得更加重要。

Betsy Z. Cohen

創辦人 / 董事長，*The Bancorp*
大都會歌劇院董事，亞洲協會董事
名譽董事，大都會博物館

My own interest in Asia has been stimulated by How Man's work. He tells me stories of what was and what is. Thus, he allows me to understand the great changes being experienced throughout Asia not only economically and politically but in the ways in which communities, people and nature change. The graphic nature of his descriptions brings to life parts of the Asian landscape I never knew existed. How Man is creating a compendium of stories and a record of impact which will serve us better and better as time moves on.

Betsy Z. Cohen

Founder/Chairman, The Bancorp
Trustee, Metropolitan Opera, Asia Society
Hon Trustee, Metropolitan Museum

作者序

在伊洛瓦底江的上游為這兩本書寫序似乎是很合適的。我們的營地在海拔 3900 公尺處，離河流真正的源頭只有幾公里。但是從這裡到源頭還需要再爬升海拔 1000 公尺，加上只能徒步行走，確實是一段艱難的路。

有一位中國的遙感探測專家，他依據衛星影像，指出伊洛瓦底江的源頭是一個高山源湖。事實上，我和團隊在四個月前已經到過那個湖，這趟我們再次回來是為了尋找注入那個湖的一條溪流。

我們的 NASA 衛星影像專家馬丁〈Martin Ruzek〉告訴我，一年之中有 6 個月的雪融時期可以看到另外一條長達 1.4 公里的溪流，而這條溪流會注入那個高山源湖。因此，若只有抵達到那個源湖對我們來說是不夠的。我們知道一定要再回來確認這條亞洲最偉大的河流之一的源頭。這趟旅程在自然一書的最後一章裡有所描述。

PREFACE

It seems appropriate that I am writing this preface at the upper reaches of the Irrawaddy River. Our basecamp, at an altitude of 3900 meters, is only a few short kilometers from the actual river source. But to reach it from here will require some serious hiking and a climb of another 1000 meters in elevation.

According to one of China's foremost remote sensing experts who defined river sources through satellite images, an alpine source lake is the geographic source of the Irrawaddy. My team and I reached the source lake only four months ago, but are now returning to explore a stream that feeds the lake.

Our own NASA satellite image expert Martin Ruzek revealed to me that, during six months of the year when the snow was melted, it would expose another stream, 1.4 kilometers in length, feeding the lake. Thus reaching the source lake is simply not good enough for us. We know we must return to verify the ultimate source of one of the most important rivers of Asia. That journey is described in the last chapter of the book on nature.

這樣的舉動無疑地彰顯了探險的精神，為了得到這個世界的真正知識，我們必需灌注更多的執著和努力，即使這個知識僅是個很微小的細節。在我們抵達依洛瓦底江源頭的那個月裡我同時也書寫了另一篇在紐約市中心的體驗。那是完全不一樣的世界，不一樣的高度，關於帝國大廈。而這也正好呈現了人類生命中多樣的眼界與經歷，而探險正是這些經歷與知識的邊沿。

這兩本書，一本關於自然，另一本聚焦文化，是我系列書的第 19 和第 20 本，記錄我在實地的工作狀況以及旅途上的回顧。每個篇章都是致力於探險的累積，不斷地向前追求新知中，也同時追述我們保育工作項目的後續。

這兩本書裡的故事除了發生在中國之外，還有關於其他鄰近國家的記述，我希望帶著讀者跟著我到另一塊陸地和海洋，一起去看看這些我曾經走訪過的地區。希望你會喜歡這些旅程，當我的探險夥伴，與我一同經歷我所經歷。

黃效文

CERS 創辦人 / 會長

日期　二零一七年十月二日

This type of effort epitomizes what exploration spirit is about, an obsession and dedication to even the smallest details in order to attain additional knowledge about our physical world. Another piece, written within a month before reaching the Irrawaddy source, is diabolically different, in the heart of New York City, and to a very different height, that of the Empire State Building. It represents the diversity of our human experience, as exploration is precisely about probing the edges of experience and knowledge.

These two volumes of books, one on nature, the other on culture, are the 19th and 20th in a series chronicling my work in the field as well as my reflections during those journeys. They are the culmination of our perseverance in exploration and constant pursuit of knowledge, and at times recount our follow-on conservation endeavors.

The stories in these two books cover more than China and her neighboring countries, bringing our readers to regions I have had the opportunity to visit on other continents and even oceans. I hope you enjoy these journeys as you travel by my side.

Wong How Man
Founder/President CERS
October 2, 2017

進入印度的側門與後門

SIDE DOOR, THEN BACK DOOR, INTO INDIA

Kalewa, Myanmar – August 18, 2016

進入印度的側門與後門

緬甸有很長的國界連著中國與印度。最近，在緬甸和印度有一小段邊界情勢有點緊張，也因此，驅使我去探索那個區域。*HM Explorer* 在欽敦江邊的葛禮瓦下錨，我們六人搭上廂型車，前往大約四小時車程外印度邊界上的德穆鎮。德穆鎮的對面是印度小鎮莫雷，這是二戰期間日軍往北推進緬甸時，大量英軍撤往印度的地方。但邊界市集已經關閉了好幾天，邊境關卡附近所有店家也都空空的。

看守關卡的男子在我過橋之後示意我回去。最近發生的動亂使得邊界市集暫時被關閉了。原來是因為有個緬甸青年他的母親是印度人，最近被殺害。為了防止進一步的殺戮與報復，他們暫時停止市場營業。我們的司機是個相當在地的人，他知道該如何進入印度的側門。

我們迅速開車穿過一座樹林，並跨越一座舊英國時代的軍用橋梁，這讓我們匿蹤越界進入印度。沒有巡邏隊或邊界管制站，只有半開的紅白色桿子橫過路面。路邊有

Kalewa, Myanmar – August 18, 2016

SIDE DOOR, THEN BACK DOOR, INTO INDIA

Myanmar has a long border with both China and India. At the moment, the situation along one small section of the long Myanmar border with India is a little tense, so naturally, I wound up exploring that region. Our boat the HM Explorer anchored at Kalewa along the Chindwin River. With a van, six of us headed for the Indian border at the town of Tamu, around four hours away. Across the border is Moreh, a small Indian town. This was the location where, during WWII, the massive British army retreated into India as the Japanese pushed north into Burma. But today the border market has been closed for days and all shops near the gate are empty.

A man guarding the gate motioned for me to turn back once I crossed. A recent riot had prompted the temporary closure of the border market. Apparently a young Burmese man whose mother was Indian had been recently killed. In order to prevent further killings and revenge, the market was suspended. But our driver, someone quite local, knew a side door into India.

We quickly drove through some wooded area, and there it was, an old British era army bridge. It provided our stealthy crossing into India. There was no

Clouds crossing Kalew / 越過葛禮瓦大橋的雲霧

一面告示牌用英文表示歡迎我們來到印度。許多機車騎士來來去去，這一定是個特殊的捷徑。當官方設立的邊界關閉時，非官方的管道往來還是照常。這段邊界的情況並不罕見，在世界上許多地方都同樣可以看到。

這時我們開上一條泥土路——名符其實的泥土，路兩旁散落著堆積的垃圾。不久前我們才經過幾棟剛粉刷過的白色建築，那是印度海關房舍，房舍附近有幾輛等著裝貨的卡車。地面上堆著大布袋，裡面裝著緬甸出口到印度的大宗之一，檳榔。我們沒有停留，繼續驅前，經

Market closed at Moreh / 關閉中的莫雷市場

border immigration or patrol, only a half-opened red and white bar across the road. A sign in English welcomes us into India. This must be a special by-pass as many motorcyclists were traveling back and forth. So what if the official border crossing was closed? The unofficial channel was conducting business as usual. That however was not unique to this border, but normal for many parts of the world.

Now we were on a dirt road - literally dirt, as large tracks of trash littered both sides of this road. Soon we passed the freshly painted Indian Customs House, an ensemble of white-washed buildings. Nearby were trucks waiting

過一座堆著沙包的臨時哨所。有幾個值勤的士兵，把步槍扔在一旁，看起來一派輕鬆。我假裝看著反方向，只用眼角觀察他們。

繼續往前 500 公尺左右，道路盡頭有一座包覆鐵絲網的閘門。如果有人要折返緬甸，這是官方隘口的另一端。短短十五分鐘，我們繞過了整個官方邊界設施從側門進入了印度。

比起緬甸，印度這邊的房屋周圍都是垃圾，看起來貧窮破爛多了。然而，閘門附近的印度教寺廟卻很乾淨。透過寺廟門口，我看到裡面有許多盛裝的印度婦女與兒童。我們停下車子小心翼翼地窺視裡面，有幾位婦女示意我們進去加入正在進行的慶典活動，於是我們脫了鞋走進廟裡。其他人示意我們去拿些食物吃，但我們禮貌地拒絕了，走向人群聚集的舞台。

這天是陰曆十五月圓日，對他們來說是個特殊的日子，婦女和孩子們的穿著鮮艷亮麗。信徒們向眾神致敬，祈求廟的新增建工程能夠順利完成建造。為了這個動工儀式，他們還特別從仰光的印度教丁茵寺拿了些泥土過來。有兩名信徒在旁邊分發編織手環給前來參加慶典的人。大家都穿上最好的衣服。印度人的好客與上相讓我

to be loaded. Huge bags were piled up on the ground, each stuffed with betel nuts, a popular export from Myanmar to India. Without stopping, we drove on and past an occasional army guard house with sandbags. A few soldiers were on duty but they looked relaxed, with rifles laid to the side. I pretended to look the other way, observing the soldiers only with the end of my eyes.

In another 500 meters or so, our road ended at a gate with barbed wire. This was the other end of the official crossing, if one were to head back toward Myanmar. Within a matter of fifteen minutes, we had circumvented the entire border official installations and entered India through a side door.

Compared to Myanmar, houses here on the Indian side looked far more poor and dilapidated with much trash lying around. The Hindu temple near the gate, however, was very clean. Through its opening, I could see many well-dressed Indian women and children inside. We stopped our van and peeked in gingerly. Some women gestured for us to enter and join in the festivities just underway. Off went our shoes and we entered the temple. Others motioned for us to go get some food. We declined politely and moved toward a stage where crowds were gathering.

The women and children were dressed most colorfully. This was the 15th Day on the lunar calendar and a full moon, a special day for them. They were paying homage to their gods in preparation of the safe construction of a new wing

驚訝，不僅沒人介意被拍攝，事實上不分男女，很多人都樂意為我們擺上好看的姿勢。

我有點擔心邊界巡邏隊隨時有可能衝進來逮捕我們這些非法入境者。畢竟，軍營就在寺廟外幾步之遙。我們只逗留了半小時就繼續上路。我其實很想繼續開到大約四小時車程外的城市因帕爾。但月圓時也是做壞事最可能暴露的時候，所以我想還是安全至上。我指示司機回緬甸去。闖人家派對是一回事，被捕可是另一回事！

Women gather / 婦女聚會

to the temple. To do so, some soil from a Hindu temple at Thanlyin in Yangon was also brought here to commence the ceremony. Two religious men were on hand to offer woven wrist bracelets to those attending the festival. Everyone was in their best dress. I was surprised that the Indians were so hospitable, as well as photogenic. No one minded being photographed. In fact, many posed for us, both men and women.

I felt a bit of apprehension that any moment the border patrol might start storming in to apprehend us I.I's (Illegal Immigrants). After all, the garrison was only steps away from the Temple. We lingered for just half an hour and then went on our way. I would have loved to continue driving to Imphal, a city some four hours away. But full moon is also when devilish deeds may be exposed, so I thought I should play safe. I instructed the driver to head back into Myanmar. Crashing a party is one thing, being crashed is something else!

Once across the iron bridge, we drove past the Myanmar guard house as if nothing had happened and left Tamu in a hurry. Consulting my satellite images, I had other plans in mind, just further down the road. Twenty or so kilometers out of town, a policeman stood in the middle of the road and waved for us to stop our van. From the serious look on his face, we knew something was wrong. He was talking into his mobile phone. On the other end of line was the border immigration officer. We were noticed by the border guards of Myanmar, as we did not stop and register upon entry.

一過了鐵橋，我們若無其事地經過緬甸哨所，迅速地離開德穆。我參考我的衛星影像，心裡另有打算。大約出城廿公里後，有個警察站在路中央揮手示意我們停車。從他的嚴肅表情看來，我們感覺到一定有甚麼不對勁。他對著手機講話，電話另一端是邊界移民官。我們被緬甸的邊界衛兵發現了，因為我們沒有停下來登記入境。

我們故作輕鬆地下了車。我們的緬甸經理珊卓是個迷人又強勢的美女。我聽著她用自信的語氣回答警察問題。不久她接過電話向移民官解釋。我不太在乎她編了什麼故事，只要我們能通過這個路障。珊卓給警察一份我們的外國乘客名單跟護照資料，狀況暫時「搞定」。差點陷入絕境之後我們匆忙地離開。

我們在早晨七點下船瘋狂的趕往印度邊界，現在已經是下午了。衛星影像告訴我將會有一大段約 15 公里的路緊貼著印度邊界，有些地方距離只有 400 公尺甚至更近。這對頑固的探險家是好消息。三年前，我們步行進入印度只為了從這個點看一眼，但沒抵達另一側的任何村莊。這次，我決心碰碰運氣。

我從衛星影像看到三個村莊，一大兩小，就在緬甸側的路邊不遠處。隱約有條小路通往我們想要探訪的大村子。

We got out of the van casually as if nothing was the matter. Sandra, our Myanmar manager is a dashing and assertive young lady. I heard her answering the police questions with a confidant voice. Soon she took over the phone and was explaining to the immigration officer her story. I didn't quite care what story she was telling, just that we should get through this barricade. Momentarily the situation was "handled" as Sandra gave the police a copy of our list of foreign passengers and passport information. We took off in a bigger hurry after that near impasse.

We left our boat at 7am in the morning on this mad rush to the Indian border, and now we are well into the afternoon. Satellite images told me that a long stretch of about 15 kilometers of our road would hug the national border with India, at times separated by 400 meters or less. This was good news for a defiant explorer. Three years ago, we hiked into India just to have a look from this point, but did not reach any villages on the other side. This time, I was

Friendly man / 友善的男子

Hands of beauty / 漂亮的手

於是我們將車停在小路盡頭，並前往路邊的商店詢問。店裡剛好有兩部機車，因此我們迅速議價，請了兩位男子來載我們四個人，每部車後座擠兩個人，前往村子。

穿過矮小樹叢並且偶爾泥濘的一公里小路之後，我們來到三個相鄰印度村莊中最大的 Chang Pol 村；這裡所謂大也不過十五棟房子。我預期印度這邊的村子會是貧窮髒亂的，但是出乎意料，這個村子包括周圍地區都非常的乾淨，幾乎一塵不染。

Rosemary's father / 蘿絲瑪莉的父親

determined to push my luck.

I could see from the satellite images that three villages, one large and two small, lay a short distance from the Burmese side of the road. A faint trail led to the larger village, the target of my visit. We stopped at the trail head and inquired at the village store. There were two motorcycles in the shop and we quickly negotiated for two men to take four of us, two passengers packed onto the back of each motorcycle, and headed for the village.

After about one kilometer through some bushy and at times muddy trails, we reached Chang Pol, the largest of the three neighboring Indian villages; large in this case meaning fifteen houses. I had expected another poor and dirty village on the Indian side. But to my surprise, the village, including the surrounding grounds, was extremely clean and almost spotless.

A young girl dressed in an embroidered green Indian tunic was perched on the balcony of one house. We stopped and chatted. Sandra naturally spoke Burmese to her, given that the village is only one kilometer from the Myanmar side of the road. We were surprised that she spoke back in perfect English. It turned out Rosemary was one of seven teachers in the local school, a primary school that supports all three nearby Indian villages, with maybe sixty students.

有一個穿著繡花綠色印度罩衫的年輕女孩站在陽台上，於是我們停下來跟她聊天。珊卓很自然地用緬語跟她說話，因為這村子距離緬甸只有一公里。但令人驚訝的是，女孩竟然用純熟的英語回答。原來蘿絲瑪莉是當地小學的七位老師之一，附近三個印度村莊大約有六十個學生。

蘿絲瑪莉的膚色和五官比較接近緬甸／中國人而非印度人。其實，整村的人都像她這樣。「我們是餅乾人。」蘿絲瑪莉說。「蛤？『餅乾』是指怪獸餅乾 (Cookie Monster) 嗎？」我問道。「是 Kuki（欽族）。拼成 K-U-K-I。」蘿絲瑪莉趕緊糾正我。他們沒有電視，但是有從印度那邊接過來的電力。附近有太陽能板，還有些小太陽能裝置在地面上收集陽光。這些小手電筒是印度政府提供的。

蘿絲瑪莉 23 歲，未婚。她說大多數女孩滿十六歲左右就嫁人。我們問她為什麼還單身。「村裡沒有好男人。」她回答。「我是老么，這是我哥哥。」蘿絲瑪莉指著一個有妻兒的年輕人說。他們看來完全不像印度人，我要求看哥哥的身分證。他立刻進屋子拿出他的印度身分證——賈米倫・馬特。上面寫著他 1998 年出生。

「妳不是說妳是老么嗎？」我問蘿絲瑪莉她和哥哥的年

Rosemary's complexion and features are closer to Burmese/Chinese than native to India. In fact, the entire village is similar in ethnicity. "We are the cookie people," Rosemary said. "Huh? 'Cookie' like in Cookie Monster?" I asked. "Kuki. K-U-K-I is the spelling," Rosemary quickly corrected me. They didn't have television, but electricity was fed through wires brought in from the Indian side. Solar panels were around, as well as some tiny solar devices collecting sunlight on the ground. These small flashlights were provided by the Indian government.

Rosemary is 23 and not yet married. She said most girls get married around sixteen years of age. We asked how come she's still single. "There's no good man in the village," she answered. "I am the youngest and here is my brother," Rosemary said while pointing to a young man with his wife and baby. As they did not look Indian at all, I asked to see the brother's I.D. He promptly entered the house and brought out his Indian citizen card - Jamminlen Mate. It said he was born in 1998.

"Didn't you say you are the youngest?" I asked Rosemary regarding the discrepancy of the age difference between her and her brother. "Yes, my brother was actually born in 1989 but when they registered him, they reversed the two numbers," mused Rosemary. I asked about local animals and in a moment her father brought out a rifle to show us that he could still hunt.

齡為何矛盾。「對，我哥其實生於 1989 年，他們登記的時候，把兩個數字弄反了。」蘿絲瑪莉笑道。我問起關於當地動物的事，一會兒她的父親拿出一把步槍告訴我們他還能夠打獵。

接著她帶我們去看相當原始的校舍，用塑膠布隔開不同年級的學生。我答應會寄一些英文書來給學生，並詢問這裡的地址。不久郵差 Limkhojam 先生戴著帽子出現。這個中年人告訴我們村子的地址，並向我們保證他一收到書就會交給學校。所有郵件都會從印度那邊送來，他們使用的唯一貨幣是盧比，不是緬甸的緬元。

「我們這個村裡都是天主教徒。」蘿絲瑪莉對我透露。接著她帶我們去看他們的教堂。外面有三塊舊墓碑，可能是以前神父的墳墓。「每年復活節和聖誕節，會有神父來作彌撒。」蘿絲瑪莉告訴我。我們告別之前，她的家人用自家後院樹上現採現榨的青檸汁招待我們。

「我們面對的一切都來自印度這邊。」蘿絲瑪莉斷言。他哥哥也證實他們對印度的忠誠，即使他們地理位置其實是比較接近緬甸。「最近官方邊界因為兩國之間的小衝突被關閉。」蘿絲瑪莉進一步透露。我也聽說過疆界爭議，看到路上緬甸軍營附近有演習與調動。顯然，我

Next she showed me the rather primitive school house, with plastic sheets partitioning the different grades of students. I promised to send some English books for primary students and asked for the address. Soon the Postman, Mr Limkhojam, showed up wearing a cap. The middle-aged man dictated their village address and assured us that once the books were received, he would deliver them to the school. All mail would come through the Indian side, and the only currency they use is rupees, not the Kyats of Myanmar.

"We are all Catholic here in these villages," Rosemary revealed to me. Next she showed us their Spartan church. Three old tombstones stood outside, probably graves of priests of the past. "Every Easter and Christmas, a priest comes to say Mass," Rosemary assured me. Before we parted, her family treated each of us to a cup of juice from limes freshly picked and squeezed from the tree in their backyard.

"Everything we deal with is from the Indian side," Rosemary asserted. His brother also confirmed their dedication to India, despite their geographical closeness to Myanmar. "Lately the official border has been closed due to some border skirmishes between the two countries," Rosemary further revealed. I too had heard of some boundary disputes and saw along the way near the Myanmar Army barracks some military exercises and maneuvers. Obviously, we should beat a retreat before being sealed off on the Indian side.

們該趁被困在印度之前趕緊撤退才是。

不像分割韓國超過半世紀的北緯 38 度線，這段邊界是南北走向。但我們現在距離北緯 23.5°——北回歸線不遠。這條線有明確定義，路邊那面水泥牆上的標示，跟我的 iPad 上伽利略地理程式的 GPS 指數完全吻合。這與亨利 · 米勒寫的同名書籍不同，美國最高法院曾經審理是否需將該書列為色情出版品。（最後被判定為優良文學！）

如同翁山蘇姬此刻正在中國訪問的談話，我到印度的短暫探訪也提醒了我們，緊鄰在一起的國家是無法搬移他們的土地與人民的。不像航空母艦這類人造島嶼，隨著國家利益和優先順序可以在大洋之間移動，共有邊界的國家必須學習和平相處。歷史會證明，只有和平相處，大家才都有共繁榮的一天。

Emblem of hope　/希望的標誌

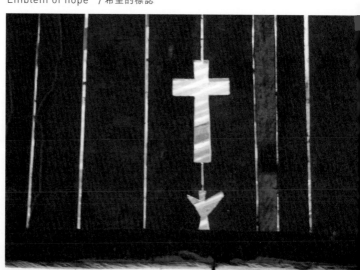

Unlike the 38th Parallel which has divided Korea for over half a Century, this border runs north to south. But we were now just a short distance from 23.5°N latitude - the Tropic of Cancer. The line was well defined, marked by a decorated cement wall along the road, which corresponded perfectly with the GPS reading on my iPad Galileo geo-program. This is quite unlike the book by the same name authored by Henry Miller, which required a ruling by the US Supreme Court as to whether it was pornographic or not. (In the end it was ruled to be fine literature!)

Like the dialogue and visit of Aung San Suu Kyi to China at this very moment, my brief visit to India was a reminder that neighboring countries cannot move their land and people away from each other. Unlike man-made islands in the form of aircraft carriers, which can be moved from one ocean to another when national interests or priorities change, nations sharing a border must learn to live with each other. History will show that, with peaceful cooperation, everyone can prosper.

Established 1947 / 設立於 1947 年

Rosemary of India / 印度的蘿絲瑪莉
Inside church / 教堂內部

Jamminlen with ID and family / 賈米倫拿著身分證與家人
Village church / 村裡的教堂

八公頃豐富的虛無

EIGHT HECTARES OF PLENTIFUL NOTHING

Maoyon River, Palawan – October 2, 2016

八公頃豐富的虛無

星辰閃耀，但我附近長到三樓高的水筆仔樹也閃爍著光亮。我納悶——聖誕節提早來了嗎？

天黑後不久，才晚上八點我就睡了，然後在凌晨一點醒來。霎時有隻螢火蟲飛過我剛才睡覺的漂浮碼頭，加入其他閃爍的光點。螢火蟲一定是徹夜開跳舞派對吧。雌蟲會點亮尾燈靜止等待，吸引雄蟲來會合交配。

森林的大合唱活過來了 —— 這是所有夜行昆蟲演出的現場交響樂。牠們或許對我們沒沒無聞，但都是動物界的明星藝人。連魚都跳出來加入，在空中翻滾掉回水中濺起水花。我在黑暗中看不到牠們，但仍想像得出每個歡愉的跟斗。

現在一定是退潮。小小的招潮蟹，與大隻泥蟹，都成群出來了，這種泥蟹可以長到三公斤重。昨天稍早，我看到兩種蟹爬出沙洞，離我們綁在岸邊的漂浮碼頭只有幾步之遙。一種是亮橘紅色，殼上有眼球狀斑點，兩隻眼

Maoyon River, Palawan – October 2, 2016

EIGHT HECTARES OF PLENTIFUL NOTHING

The stars are sparkling, but my nearby mangrove tree, rising to three story height, is also flickering with lights. I wonder - has Christmas come early?

I had gone to bed at 8 pm soon after it got dark, and now I am awake at 1 am. Momentarily a firefly flies across the floating dock where I had slept and joins the other flickering lights. The fireflies must be partying and dancing through the night. Females are known to sit and wait with their tail-lights on, attracting a male to rendezvous and mate.

The chorus of the forest has come alive – live symphony staged by all the insects of the night. They may be nameless to us, but are celebrity star performers of the animal world. Even the fish jump into action, flipping in the air and splashing back into the water. Without seeing them in darkness, I can still imagine each joyous summersault.

It must be low tide. The tiny fiddler crab, as well as huge mud crab, which at times grow to three kilos, are out in droves. Earlier yesterday, I saw two types of crabs coming out of their sand holes, just steps away from our floating dock

睛像天線般高高凸起。另一種蟹有黃白色的螯，小螯不斷揮舞著清理大螯，像拉小提琴的弓，因此得名 *Fiddler Crab*（小提琴手蟹）。

就在昨天，我們團隊在沿岸看到幾隻鱷魚。所以似乎可以斷定牠們晚上也很忙，在我們人類較少干擾時進食或單純玩耍。

「嗷嗚」安靜了約十秒鐘，然後又傳出「嗷嗚」。這個叫聲偶爾透過夜空傳來。有時感覺就在十米外，其他時候逐漸遠離到幾百公尺，但仍清晰可聞。喬絲琳說那是一種特殊生物，像異形很可怕。有人說它有第三隻眼。據說會對人類下咒然後殺害。我聽到這聲音的第一晚，設法模仿與回應。喬絲琳趕緊阻止我，警告說可能招霉運。她似乎真的很擔心。

以聲波傳遞的速度，我想那一定是某種夜行鳥類，在樹木之間飛行。稍後漫遊過這座叢林的洛伊證實了這點，他也說那是鳥。或許是某種鳥類，但喬絲琳仍堅持這種鳥或動物身上有惡靈。人的想像力常常是無窮的。

洛伊對這些森林瞭若指掌。他提議清理這片濕地，這是

tied to the shore. One type is bright orange red, with eye-like markings on its shell, behind two real eyes sticking high up like two antennas. The other crab sported yellowish white claws, with the tiny claw frequently fiddling and cleaning the larger one, like a bow playing a violin, thus the name Fiddler Crab.

Just yesterday, our team saw several crocodiles along the shore. So it seems safe to say that they too must be busy at night, feasting themselves or simply playing when we humans are less intrusive.

"Awoooo," then silence for maybe ten second, then "Awoooo," once again. This howling came occasionally throughout the night. At times it felt like it was just ten meters away, and other times it went off gradually into a distance of hundreds of meters, yet still distinctly audible. Jocelyn said these are a special kind of being, very scary, like aliens. Some say it has a third eye. They are supposed to cast spells on people and kill. On my first night hearing such sounds, I tried to imitate and answer. Jocelyn stopped me quickly, warning that it may bring bad luck. She seemed obviously and seriously concerned.

At the rate the sound traveled, I thought it must be some kind of a nocturnal bird, moving from tree to tree. Later this was confirmed by Roy who has roamed this jungle forest. He too said it is a bird. A bird of sorts perhaps, but Jocelyn still insisted that this bird or animal carries ill spirit. Imagination is

Red Crab / 紅蟹 ・Fiddler Crab / 招潮蟹

我們在巴拉望取得設立基地的八公頃土地的一部分。洛伊說我們的土地上有一群猴子，當然也有些巨蜥，當地人稱之為 Bayawak，我雖然只是新手生物學家，但也已經熟悉了這種巨蜥的叫聲。白鷺鷥很多，靜靜沿著河岸走來走去等待獵物上門。有隻巨大的翠鳥，是這裡的常客或居民，也高踞在水筆仔樹上等待牠的下個獵物，無論是蜻蜓或魚。

昨天稍早，洛伊先帶我看他設置的捕鱷陷阱，再帶我進入茂密的森林到一個表面爬滿蜜蜂的巨大野蜂巢那兒。他提議隔天清晨幫我收集一點蜂蜜，因為涼爽的時候蜜蜂比較不活躍，多多少少比較無害。他說蜜蜂不會喜歡

often, quite boundless.

Roy knows these forests like the back of his hands. He offered to clear and clean the wetland which is part of the eight hectares that we have acquired to set up a base here in Palawan. It was he who said our land hosts a group of monkeys. Certainly there are some Monitor lizards, Bayawak as the locals call them, the large reptile whose calling sound is now familiar to me, despite being a novice of a naturalist. Egrets are plentiful, waiting for their catch by quietly strolling up and down the river banks. A giant kingfisher, a regular visitor or perhaps a resident here, perched on the tall mangrove tree waiting for its next prey, be it a dragonfly or a fish.

Earlier yesterday, Roy showed me first a trap he had set up to catch crocodile, then led me inside the dense forest to a huge wild bee hive covered with bees on the outside. He offered to collect the honey for me in the morning. When it is cool the bees are less active and more or less harmless. He said the bees won't like his sweaty, day-time smell, with sweat, so he should come back clean in the morning.

Our eight hectares fronts a very pristine river, Maoyon River, which literally cuts the long island of Palawan into two halves, from west to east. By setting ourselves up strategically here, we can study the river and freshwater life all the way up to some limestone hills, at the foothills of the World Heritage Un-

他陽光下汗臭的氣味，何況還有淋漓的汗水，所以他最好一清早身上乾淨時再回來。

我們的八公頃面對一條很原始的河流 Maoyon，從西往東名符其實把長形的巴拉望島切成兩半。我們策略性駐紮在此，不僅可以研究河流和淡水生物，還能夠一路追溯到幾座石灰岩山丘，就位在世界遺產地底河流的山腳下。我們的探洞團隊到時可以探索該區域的洞穴，同時讓生物學家專注在其他野生動物與生態議題。距離河口只有兩個河彎的這塊地，離洪達灣的廣闊海洋可能還不到半公里。這裡是淡水與鹹水融合之處，因此同時提供了這兩種生物的棲地。從這裡，我們的 HM Explorer II 可以出海，研究海洋生物、珊瑚礁、環礁上築巢的鳥類，還有許多島上的人類生活。

這塊地，與這裡的寧靜給了我時間去思考與反省。八公頃是什麼概念？對我們比較關心與熟悉平方呎的香港人，等於八十萬平方呎，或一千戶各 800 平方呎的公寓！世界都是相對的，最重要的是相關性。在我們擁擠的城市裡，平方呎成為人生最重要的單位。

但在巴拉望這裡，英畝或公頃才是常用的單位。進一步說，例如在我擔任過首席顧問的新疆阿爾金山自然保護

derground River. Our caving team can then explore caves of the region while our biologists focus on other wildlife and ecological issues. Our land is two bends from the estuary and perhaps less than half a kilometer from the vast ocean of Honda Bay. Here is where salt water merges with freshwater, thus providing a habitat for both types of life forms. From here, our HM Explorer II boat can sail the blue ocean, studying marine life, coral reefs, bird nesting atoll, as well as human life on the many islands.

Our land here and its peacefulness give me a moment to think and reflect. So

Roy getting honey / 洛伊取蜂蜜

區，我們使用更大的公制單位「平方公里」來計算。那個保護區佔地四萬五千平方公里，比台灣大了將近一萬平方公里，但是那裡只住了十幾戶人家。

過去我利用 NASA 從太空拍攝的影像，那壯觀的全景提供了國家、大陸，甚至整個地球上完全不同的參考點。這一點讓我們對所存在的這個世界有比較超脫的觀點，有時候也能用來解讀自己的人生哲學。

那是早在 Google Earth 或 GPS 變得家喻戶曉的時代前。很不幸地，對某些人來說我們的觀點永遠是微不足道、渺小又自我中心。但無疑，中國古諺「井蛙觀天」可能具體反映了某些城市人多麼心胸狹隘。我們不俯瞰我們的地球，連無人機都不用。我們反而蔑視其他人，包括闖入他們的隱私，把情況戲劇化、煽情化以激起大眾情緒。

CERS 很高興取得了這八公頃的虛無。這對某些人或許沒什麼價值，但當我在夜裡醒來，我覺得這真是最珍貴的八公頃虛無。現在我們終於有機會，能以適當的方式為它增添價值了。研究、保育和教育價值正是探險學會在可見的未來能帶給這個新地方的。

what is eight hectares? For those of us in Hong Kong who are more concerned and familiar with only square footage, it is 800,000 square feet, or 1,000 apartments of 800 square foot each! The world is all relative, and very much about relevancy. In our crowded city, square footage would be of utmost importance to a person's life.

But here in Palawan, acres or hectares are the denominations of choice. Going further, for example at the Arjin Mountain Nature Reserve in Xinjiang where I was formerly Chief Advisor, we calculate by an even larger matric, in square kilometers. The reserve is 45,000 square kilometers in area, almost 10,000 square kilometers larger than Taiwan, yet with only a dozen or so families living within it.

Kingfisher on mangrove tree / 水筆仔樹上的翠鳥

有些人可能會混淆「無價」和「無價值」。但對我們來說，無價反而代表一切！借用禪宗的說法，空即一切！

Floating dock abode / 漂浮碼頭兼住所

When I used to work with NASA Space Shuttle images, the spectacular high view offered totally different reference points of a country, a continent, and even our globe. Thus we can have a more elevated perspective of our world, and at times interpret our own philosophy of life.

This was long before Google Earth or GPS became a household word. Unfortunately for some of us, our viewpoint will forever continue to be minuscule, microscopic and self-centered. No doubt, the Chinese classical idiom, "A Frog looking at the sky from the bottom of a well", can be a valid reflection of how small minded some of us city dwellers have become. We don't look down on our earth, not even with a drone. Instead, we look down on others, including intruding into their privacy, dramatizing and sensationalizing situations to arouse public sentiments and create relevancy.

For now we at CERS are pleased to have acquired eight hectares of emptiness. To some it may seem nothing of value. But I woke up in the night to feel that this is a most precious eight hectares of nothingness. We now have a chance to add value to it, hopefully with sensitivity. Research, conservation and education values are what CERS can bring to this new site in the foreseeable future.

Some people may mix up priceless and worthless. Instead, for some of us, priceless means everything! Borrowing from Zen, emptiness is wholeness.

A PERSONAL EDUCATION/ LEARNING REFLECTIONS

個人教育與學習的反省

Zhongdian, Yunnan – October 12, 2016

個人教育與學習的反省 向「不」說不

如果今天說我是「受過教育的人」，或許會被認為有些爭議，但也不盡言過其實。畢竟，我從母校接受的榮譽博士學位似乎支持這個說法。如果我剛離開高中或大學時說同一句話，恐怕就不太能讓人接受，即使是我自己。

在校時，我向來不是傑出的學生。我生平的專長或天命從來不是念書，更別提小時候了。高中時期，我放學後常被留校察看。即使如此，我仍自認一輩子都是個學生——終身努力學習的人。

中國諺語「學海無涯」是我不僅贊同，而且奉行的座右銘。追根究底向來是我的生命泉源。所有小孩子都是這樣，但不知何故我直到青春期、成年和現在同樣有爭議的「晚年」都還保持著這種心態。

A PERSONAL EDUCATION / LEARNING REFLECTIONS

Saying "no" to "No"

If I say I am "an educated person" today it might be considered debatable, but not altogether an overstatement. After all, the honorary doctorate that I received from my alma mater seems to support that statement. If I said the same when I was just out of high school or college, it would not sit well, even with myself.

At school, I was never a student of distinction. Studying was never my forte or vocation throughout life, let alone during my formative years. By high school, detention class was my habitual home after school. Despite that, I still consider myself a perpetual student - someone who is trying to learn throughout life.

The Chinese idiom, "Learning has no horizon," is a motto I not only endorse, but practice. That inquisitiveness has been my life-spring. This is true with all young children, but somehow it stayed with me as I enter puberty, adulthood,

叛逆，適當又機靈的叛逆，或許最能形容我受教育的體驗。雖然現在我教我們的實習生不要接受別人說「不」，在小學或高中裡太早實踐，可是要付出代價的，尤其對外表現出來的話。所以我很久以前就學會了用我自己的低調方式向「不」說不。

我到處實驗說「不」的旅程，有時候會帶來實際或嚴重的後果。所以，現在我進一步修正給實習生的教導：「如果你能承受後果的話，就放手去做」。

我的幼稚園是中華基督教禮賢會在香港區會設立的教會學校，教室就在教堂後方的兩個房間。那裡影響了我對人生的道德觀與精神歷程。老樣子，中國古諺或許有點道理。不是有句中國諺語說了嗎，「三歲定終生」。

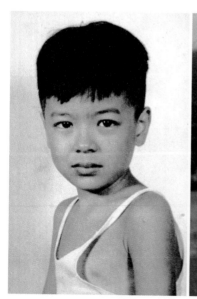

and now, again debatably, my "twilight" years.

Defiance, appropriate and tactful defiance, perhaps best characterizes my educational experience. While today I teach our interns not to take "No" as an answer, exercising that too early, while in elementary or high school, creates a price to pay, especially if exhibited outwardly. Therefore I long ago learned to say "no" to "No" in my own quiet way.

I went about experimenting on those "No" journeys, at times with real or serious consequences. For that matter, now I modify and further qualify my teaching to our interns; "Go ahead if you can afford the consequences".

My kindergarten was a mission school established by the Chinese Rhenish Church Synod with the two-room set up behind the church building. That may have played a role in setting my moral and spiritual path in life. Again, there may be some truth in ancient Chinese sayings. Another Chinese idioms states, "Three years will determine what comes at eighty".

For First Grade, I entered True Light Elementary, essentially a girl's school with some boys accepted in the lower forms. This was an extremely conservative protestant school. Girls are not allowed to curl their hair, which had to be above shoulder length, and their light blue "Cheung Sam" uniform had to be long, below the knee and half way to the ankle. As a boy, I sported white well-

Early riding lesson ／早期學騎馬

一年級時，我進了真光小學，基本上這是個女校，只收一些低年級的男學童。在這間極度保守的基督教學校裡，女生們不准燙髮，長度不能超過肩膀，她們的淺藍色「長衫」制服必須過膝，到小腿的一半。身為男生，我穿燙過的白襯衫與淡藍色及膝的短褲。

到了國中，我進入以成績優異和嚴格的愛爾蘭神父著稱

ironed shirts and light blue knee-length shorts.

For secondary school, I entered Wah Yan Kowloon, a Jesuit English college famed for its academic excellence and the discipline of the Irish priests. I entered in Primary 6, repeating a year in order to catch up with English, having come from a Chinese school. My father was a life-long science teacher at the school, known for his innovative ways of teaching and much respected by peers and students alike. He even authored the text book on Chemistry for the Hong Kong School Certificate Examination.

With my father's grace I entered into the Primary 6A class, the pinnacle of the four classes, each of 40 students. Top academic students always remain in the A class. Suffice to say from that high point, I descended to 1B, then 2C and so on and so forth until, at Form 5, I was supposed to be in the last of the five classes, in 5F. But grace was bestowed on me again, despite avoiding baptism for five years. The class was renamed 5A Arts, salvaging me some lost dignity!

By now, I had befriended many senior classmen and under-classmates, accumulating enough of a rolodex to qualify me as a future candidate for alumni president should I decide to challenge for that seat. The secret of getting to become close friends of upper and lower classmates was to be always present

的耶穌會英語學校——九龍華仁書院就讀。因為出自中文學校，我小六入學時，留級一年為了跟上英文程度。家父在該校當了一輩子科學老師，以創新教學方式聞名，很受同僚與學生們的尊重。他甚至為香港中學會考寫過一本化學教科書。

托家父的福我進了小六 A 班，四班之中最好的一班，每班有四十位學生。成績最好的學生留在 A 班，老實說我從那個高點一路跌到一年 B 班，接著二年 C 班，以此類推直到中五，我應該在五班裡面吊車尾的五年 F 班。然而即使五年來我一直逃避受洗，但老天還是可憐我，這一班改名為 5A 文科班，幫我挽回了一點失去的尊嚴！

這時候，我已經跟許多學長學弟成為朋友，累積了足夠人脈讓我競選校友會長。跟學長學弟成為好友的祕訣就是下課後留校察看，因為可以跟很多班級的人共聚一堂！

長話短說，我在威斯康辛的大學時代是另一場生存考驗，我勉強地活過了四個冷到無法形容的寒冬。那些年對我來說是最寶貴的，因為我可以選擇想要的課程。我常到大學圖書館，去找尋我的根，身為一個華人，我閱讀與學習中國歷史與當代問題。

Educated, U.S. style / 美式教育

at detention, when multiple classes all gather under one roof!

To make a long story short, my college years in Wisconsin were another sur-
vival test, at least in barely surviving four bitter winters beyond description.
Those years were most valuable for me as I was able to pick the classes and

在大學裡，我領悟到，在外國的偏遠地方身為少數民族的意義。因而讓我畢業後在漫遊中國少數民族地區時受用不盡，直到今天我持續學習與應用了這堂課四十多年。我的新聞與藝術雙學位正好符合我的好奇心，也讓我獲得用藝術表達的自由，無論透過我的照片或繪畫，甚至是我的寫作風格。

如今，我看看每年夏天加入我們探險學會的年輕實習生，回顧我自己的教育。我讚嘆他們帶來的活力。他們替今年將滿三十歲的組織增添了價值。我希望，作為回報，我們能讓實習生學習到以探險的精神，永不停止學習。

我告誡他們，「如果你的書沒念好，還是可以當個探險家。」

With parents at airport heading to US / 前往美國時與雙親攝於機場

curriculum of my choice. I frequented the university library to find out about my own roots, that of being a Chinese, both about China's history and its contemporary issues.

In college, I learned what it means to be a minority, in a remote place of a foreign country. It thus charted my future path of roaming the minority regions of China after graduation, a curriculum I have continued to study for over forty years of my life up till now. My double major in Journalism and Art was a perfect match for my inquisitiveness, as well as providing the freedom of artistic expression, be it through my photography, or drawings, and extending even into my writing style.

Today, as I observe our young interns joining us at CERS each summer, I reflect back on my own education. I am amazed at how energizing and rejuvenating their presence is. They add value to what might otherwise be an old organization that is turning 30 this year. It is my hope that, in return, we can provide our interns a taste of the spirit of exploration that leads to a life of learning with no horizon.

But I caution in telling them, "If you don't study well, you can always become an explorer."

海上跳島250公里之旅

ISLAND HOPPING 250 KILOMETERS OUT AT SEA

Palawan, Philippines - Dec 17, 2016

海上跳島 250 公里之旅

通常我的皮膚還挺光滑的，但是現在伸手摸摸自己的手臂和腿，會摸到腫塊和硬塊。我是這樣教我們的實習生的，「如果無法改變情況，那就必須改變自己的態度。」所以這幾天和這幾個鐘頭，我一直努力改變我的態度——發癢很舒服，抓癢很滿足。但是至今沒什麼效果。

我們在巴拉望最新項目的所在地被一條有紅樹林的原始河流和沼澤圍繞，這周圍的蚊子是我無法改變的狀況。未來工程完成後，我們才可以在蚊帳內得到妥善的庇護。現在，我只能寄望未來，將這八公頃的河濱土地開發成我們下個中心兼基地。

開發對我們的意義，是保存這塊天然棲地與環境。當地人說我們的土地上有一群猴子，畢尉林博士架設的第一個攝影機捕捉到的影像證實了這點，而且捕捉到的還不只有猴子，有泥蟹和許多其他介殼類物種。有隻鸛形喙的翠鳥似乎跟我們住在同一個樹林裡，還有

ISLAND HOPPING 250 KILOMETERS OUT AT SEA

I usually have fairly smooth skin, but for the moment when I run my hand over my arms and legs, I could feel bumps and lumps. I teach our intern students, "If you cannot change the situation, you must change your attitude". So for the last hours and days, I've been working hard to change my attitude – that itching feels good, and scratching provides fulfilment. It has not worked so far.

The mosquito around our latest project site here in Palawan surrounded by a pristine river of mangrove and swamp is a perpetual situation I cannot change. At least not until construction is finished and we can be sheltered properly inside netted premises. For now, my hopes are put into the future, with eight hectares of riverside land being developed into our next center/ base.

Develop, for us means preserving this natural habitat and environment. Locals said that there are a group of monkeys within our land, and Dr Bleisch's first set of camera trap images reveal just that, and more. There are mud crab as well as many other species of crustaceans. A Stork-billed Kingfisher seems

另一對生態飽受威脅的大灰啄木鳥也是。在我臨時住
所旁，有一棵高大水筆仔，夜間住著一群螢火蟲，每晚
我都能見到牠們。

我們的這塊土地跟鄰接的沼澤與濕地一定要被好好保
護。陸上房屋會依照當地風俗建造。如果我的願望能
實現，漂浮碼頭上也會蓋個簡單的住所。這真是一塊
寶地，連鑿的井都非常成功，我們在地下四十米左右
挖到泉水，湧出的水十分清澈與甘甜。

Village house / 村裡的房屋

to make our trees its home, likewise a pair of threatened Great Slaty Wood-
pecker. A tall mangrove tree next to my temporary abode hosts swarms of
fireflies at night, every night.

The swamp and wetlands within and adjacent to our premises must be accord-
ed some protection. Houses on land would be built according to local custom.
If my wishes were adhered to, some simple abodes would be built on floating
docks. It is a gem of a piece of land. Even our effort to sink a well hit a fresh-
water spring, some forty meters below, gushing out water that is both clear
and sweet.

Two turns on this river, the Maoyon, would take us downstream into the blue
ocean, our target of the next decade of work among the many coral islands
of the South China Sea, and for some, the Philippine Sea. With the recent
honeymoon between the Philippines and China, it doesn't seem to matter to
call it by either name, and the Spratly/Nan Sha are, for the moment, over the
distant horizon and a diluted, rather than disputed, issue.

The U.S./Philippines joint naval exercise is on hold. After all, such matching of
the powerful and the weak only provides a chance for the former to feel supe-
rior, with their much better equipment, hardware, and far-reaching resources.
Other partners to so-called joint alliances are simply a pawn, if not puppets.
Balancing artificial land-filled islands with moving islands like aircraft-carri-

沿著這條 *Maoyon* 河過兩個彎，就能到下游的出海口，我們往後十年的工作目標是在南中國海，某些人稱作菲律賓海。最近菲律賓與中國正處於蜜月期，這些珊瑚小島稱作什麼名字似乎不重要。此刻南沙群島在遙遠的海平線外，目前它只是個被逐漸淡化而非極具爭議的議題。

美菲海軍聯合演習暫緩了。畢竟，如此的強弱結合只會讓強者感覺更為優越，畢竟他們的裝備好的太多了，還有無遠弗屆的軟硬體資源。所謂同盟的其他夥伴，即使不是傀儡也只是棋子。以航空母艦這種移動島嶼制衡人工填海製造的島嶼，是大國的遊戲，他們輸得起戰爭，而小國連打贏一仗都承受不起。復原的時間太長太久，整個經濟幾乎確定會崩潰。

世界上已經有太多智庫，卻太少具有行動力庫。探險學會希望能多貢獻些行動。務實且具常識的思考策略，不需尖端的火箭科學，就可以告訴我們中國或其鄰國無法搬家。所以每個國家必須學習互相合作。其他所謂的友邦，一旦當國家利益改變，或還有更好的發展機會出現時，就會分手。

就像股市，我們設法在機會最恰當時多做一點甚麼，遇

ers are for the big boys. They can afford to lose a war, whereas small countries cannot afford to even win a fight. The recovery time would simply take too long while the entire economy would almost be assured to collapse.

The world already has too many Think Tanks, and too few Act Tanks. CERS hopefully will contribute to more of the latter. Real strategic yet common sense thinking, not rocket science, would reveal that China or its neighboring countries cannot be moved away. So each country must learn to work with the others. Other so-called friends will depart once their national priorities change, or when there are rosier grounds elsewhere.

Not unlike the stock market, we try to do more when opportunities are optimum, and lay low when the going gets tough. Just a few months ago, our boat permit in Palawan only allowed us to cruise around nearby Honda Bay. Now a renewed permit under a new climate would let us roam free into islands even over 200 kilometers off shore. With that in mind, we rushed out to sea before the weather turns for the worse as winter sets in with high winds and rough sea. After all, the political weatherbell is also unpredictable.

HM Explorer 2 will carry our main team, with the Jezyl, a smaller fishing boat, as escort carrying important supplies like water and fuel, not least of which is ice to keep our fresh food, much of it caught at sea, fresh. We set out at midnight, just as the tide is high enough for us to clear the sandbars and

到狀況惡化時最好保持低調。就在幾個月前，我們在巴拉望拿到的許可證只允許船隻行駛到附近的洪達灣。然而新氣象下拿到的許可證，卻可讓我們自由航行到離岸 200 公里的群島去。得知此事，我們趕緊趁天氣惡化前火速出海，因為冬天常有強風與大浪。畢竟，政治風向球也是無法預測的。

HM Explorer II 是我們航行的隊長，帶領較小的漁船傑季爾號，攜帶飲水與燃料等重要補給品，還有用來保存新鮮食物的冰塊；船上的很多新鮮食糧都是從海裡抓上來的。我們在午夜出發，潮漲得夠高我們才能通過河口灣的沙洲和淺水區。這裡也是我們有機會同時研究淡水與海水棲地多樣化魚類物種的地方。不過那要等到許久之後的未來了。今晚，我們的目標落在遙遠的海上。

到了早晨五點半，天空開始泛出一絲曙光，我們只航行了 40 公里，因為夜裡海浪變大了。但是天亮後，美麗的陽光露出，我們來到平靜的海域，坐在上層甲板 360 度地欣賞無際的的海平線。看著遠方的烏雲堆積，我慶幸暴風雨遍布在遙遠的那一片天空我同時也祈禱它們會跟我們保持距離。然而我的的禱告未能應驗，約近傍晚，我們被迫躲到船艙內，讓船隻去承受暴風雨的威力。

Distant rain / 遠方的雨

shallow water of the estuary. Here is also where there will be a chance for us to work on the diverse fish species of both freshwater and marine habitats. But that must wait far into the future. This night, our aim is also far - out at sea.

By 5:30 am, as the sky began to have a tint of the first light, we have sailed only 40 kilometers out east, as the wave got choppy during the night. But by sunrise, a beautiful sunrise, we approached a calm sea and began sitting on the upper deck to take in the full breadth of the vast ocean, a full 360 degrees of horizon. With clouds at great distance, I cherish seeing faraway rainstorm clusters at different locations, and prayed that they will stay at a distance. My prayers are not answered, and later in the afternoon, we are forced under-deck as our boat braves the full onslaught of a rainstorm.

從香港出發前,我發了信給團隊每個人,提醒大家航海者天生迷信,尤其在海上受大自然的強大力量擺佈時。一旦出海絕對不准吵架。脾氣不好的人,必須把火氣留在家裡鎖好,安全回家之後再拿出來。壞脾氣會引來大浪。這事前的警告似乎生效了,我們的航程既文明又平靜。

Cagayancillo 是這次的目的地,距離巴拉望海岸約 *200* 公里,是我的助手喬絲琳她父親祖先的世居地。最近幾趟巴拉望之旅我也逐漸跟摩西混熟。他很少有機會回到這裡,也很期待這個機會。喬絲琳六歲時離開這個島,已經三十八年沒回去過。他妹妹梅西四歲離開,也是第一次回去。船上渴望的情緒高漲,甚至連我都是,我從未搭乘 *20* 米懸臂小船出海這麼遠。

搭小船連續航行廿六小時不是件輕鬆的事。海象不穩,日出與日落更是顯得最珍貴。我們在船上過了兩晚,終於在 *Talaga* 村外下錨,大約在是凌晨兩點,岸上有幾盞閃爍的小燈。整晚我蜷縮側躺在船長旁邊的小角落,因為這艘船沒有船艙,除了七位船員,船上還有我們六位乘客。另一艘漁船載著備用設備與物資,上面也有六位船員和五位乘客;包括喬絲琳殷切想要返鄉的親戚們。

Before we embarked from Hong Kong, I sent a note to everyone in my team, reminding each and every one that seafaring people are by nature superstitious, especially when they are out at sea and feel at the mercy of a much greater being, that of nature. There must be no argument once out at sea. For those with a temper, they must keep it at home locked away, retrieving it only when they return home safely. Rough temper would bring about a rough sea. The warning seems to have worked, and our cruise was civilized and calm.

Our destination is Cagayancillo, a faraway island some 200 kilometers from the shore of Palawan. It is the ancestral home of the father of my helper Jocelyn. I have gotten to know Moises over the last few trips to Palawan. He rarely gets to go home and is looking forward to this opportunity. Jocelyn herself left the island when she was six years old and has not been back for 38 years. Her sister Mercy left when she was four and is also returning for the first time. Anxiety is high on our boat, even for me, who has never gone to sea for such a great distance in a small boat, a 20-meter outrigger.

Twenty-six hours of sailing continuously is not a small feat on a small boat. But sunrise and sunset were the most valued moments, despite at times the sea being rough. We spent two nights on board, as it is around 2am when we finally drop anchor outside Talaga village, a bay with a few tiny flickering lights on the shore. Throughout the night I have been curled sideways at my tiny corner next to the skipper, as there is no cabin for the six of us passengers,

隔天就是畢尉林博士的生日，我們航行到附近的 *Central*，又稱聖十字鎮，參觀年度遊行，七公里長的島上所有村子都會參加。學校的軍樂隊從鎮上的教堂開始，以曲折路線穿過街道慶祝，彷彿為我們的老科學家歡呼。即便這個島雖小，卻不缺教堂，好幾個教派都出席了這場盛會。

我們在一座有著破爛燈塔的偏遠島邊浮潛、釣魚。我們的船員很擅長潛水時用魚叉捕魚。一群女潛水客是喬絲琳的親戚，加入我們還抓了不少海鮮當晚餐。水很清澈，隔天我們繼續往南航行三小時，在 *Cawili* 島遇見我生平見過最清澈的海水。連我們的朋友，廿年潛水經驗

Fish of Cagayancillo / Cagayancillo 島的魚

besides a crew of seven. The other boat, the fishing boat tagged along for cau-
tion, had six more in its crew and another five passengers, relatives of Jocelyn
eager to make a visit home.

It was Dr. Bleisch's birthday the next day, and we sailed to nearby Central, or
Santa Cruz town, for the parade of the year, involving all the villages of this
7-kilometer long island. Starting from the town's cathedral, school marching
bands went through the streets in a circuitous route celebrating, as if cheering
for our ageing scientist. Despite that the island is small, there were no short-
age of churches, with several denominations represented.

We did some snorkeling as well as fishing at a remote island with a beaten-up

Fish from sea / 海裡抓的魚

的 *Sammy Lam* 都沒見過這麼碧藍又透明的海水，馬爾地夫沒有，馬來西亞沒有，泰國當然更沒有。

Cawili 島很小，退潮時僅 *1.5* 公里長，住了大約 *100* 戶人家。可想而知，島上沒有電力。政府給了 *50* 個家庭太陽能電燈，其餘的家庭完全沒燈可用。在復活節和聖誕節等重大假日，島上唯一的一家雜貨店會把僅有的一台小發電機借給教堂做彌撒。雜貨店的老闆娘名叫芙蘿拉，靠收購村民種的海草賺錢，賣到日本。我們全體在她店裡吃到了一頓像樣的早餐——泡麵加煎蛋。

Cawili 島也以「鳥島」聞名，許多種海鳥棲息在此。有很多燕鷗、海鷗、鵜鶘，和最美麗的紅腳鰹鳥。我也很喜歡觀賞綠色羽毛的翠鳥。漁民每天回來時都會過來我們船邊賣龍蝦，好幾種蟹類，蝦類，烏賊和各種石斑魚。一公斤龍蝦只賣 *350* 披索（*50* 港幣），而且隨便一隻就有二公斤。至於其他海鮮，價格更是便宜。

聽說大約卅分鐘航程外有環礁，我們隨即上路。原來那裡是本地漁民與海草種植者的基地。以前有個上面住人的沙洲島叫做 *La Rinna*，但已經消失到海中了。如今已經沒有陸地，水面上只有五、六間木製高腳屋。我們抵達時是退潮，得涉水半公里，因為船必須下錨在較遠

lighthouse. Our crew were excellent in free diving while spearing for fish. A group of women divers, relatives of Jocelyn, joined our outing and caught much for dinner. The water was crystal clear, but the next day we sailed for three more hours to the south, and at Cawili island found the clearest ocean water I've ever set my eyes on. Even our friend Sammy Lam, who has been diving for twenty years, had never seen so turquoise and transparent water, not in the Maldives, not in Malaysia, and certainly not in Thailand.

Cawili island is small, only 1.5 kilometers in length during low tide, and supports approximately 100 families. There is, to be expected, no electric power. The government has given 50 families solar lights, whereas the remaining families have no lights whatsoever. On major holidays like Easter and Christmas, the only small generator is loaned out by the only sundry shop for use in the church for saying mass. Flora is the owner and she made her money through collecting of seaweed, planted by the villagers, and destined for the Japanese market. Our entire team gets a square meal at her shop as breakfast - fried eggs over instant noodles.

Cawili island is also known popularly as Bird Island as many seabirds make it their home. There is an abundance of terns, gulls, cormorants, and most beautiful of all, the Red-footed Booby. I also enjoy seeing a green-feathered Kingfisher. Everyday, fishermen returning would stop by our boat and sell us lobster, several species of crab, prawn, cuttlefish and numerous types of

處。看到人們可以這麼簡樸地生活但卻過得挺快樂的，實在很迷人。

我們回船上吃晚餐時，有個鬍鬚男划著小船過來。他臉孔晒黑發紅，牙齒全沒了，到我們船上用粵語自我介紹。我們很驚訝阿丙是香港華人，出身筲箕灣。他一九四九年出生於漁民家庭，一輩子都住在船上。直到他十六歲跟家人發生爭執。他發誓要遠走高飛去謀生，接著不知是幸或不幸，在巴拉望蘇祿海這個偏遠

Ah Peng from Hong Kong　／香港來的阿丙

*groupa. A kilogram of lobster would sell for a meager 350 peso (HKD50), and
there seemed no shortage of 2kg ones. For other seafood, they cost an insignif-
icant pittance.*

*We heard of an atoll some thirty minutes sailing away and were soon on our
way. It turned out to be a base for local fishermen and seaweed growers.
There used to be a sandbar island called La Rinna with a small community,
but have since disappeared into the ocean. Today there is no more land, just
half a dozen or so wooden sheds on tall stilts over the water. At low tide when
we arrived, we had to walk half a kilometer through shallow water, as our boat
had to be anchored further out. It was fascinating to see how people could
subsist on so little, yet live quite happily.*

*As we returned to our boat base for dinner, a slightly bearded man showed up
in a tiny row-boat. With a fully tanned red face, and teeth all gone, he came
onto our boat and introduced himself in Cantonese. We were shocked that Ap
Peng was Hong Kong Chinese, and from Shau Kei Wan at that. He was born
in 1949 into a fishing family and had stayed on boats all his life. That is until
he was 16 years old and had an argument at home with the family. He swore
that he would go as far away as possible to make a living, and, by fortune or
misfortune, ended up for 51 years in this faraway atoll in the Sulu Sea of Palawan. From here he conducts his live seafood business, married a local, and
had four children.*

環礁住了五十一年。他在這裡做活海鮮的生意，娶了本地人，生了四個小孩。

Cawili 島距離世界自然遺產圖巴塔哈群礁只有約八十公里，見多識廣的法國探險家雅克・庫斯托（Jacques Cousteau）在晚年說過這群珊瑚礁是他見過最美的海底世界之一。管理這個區域的 Cagayancillo 島轄區也包括圖巴塔哈群礁，有權力發放難得的許可證給訪客來這個保護區。他們承諾我們，如果我們下次再來造訪，他們一定會發許可證給我們。

那晚我夢到了這個海底樂園，有最純淨的水和魚類，還有一座高更或馬龍白蘭度都沒踏上的島。突然間我看到一艘大郵輪緩緩繞過 Cawili 島的角落。甲板船上有好幾百，甚至可能上千的觀光客，穿著鮮豔的夏威夷衫和短褲，拿起相機猛拍。我突然從這惡夢中醒來，發現這裡距離世界其他地方仍有幾千公里而鬆了口氣。不過這些地方還能被保護著多久就難說了。或許到時阿丙得航海到更遠的地方去尋找屬於他的新天堂。

Cawili island is only about 80 kilometers from the World Nature Heritage Site of Tubbataha, a group of coral islands that Jacques Cousteau said late in his illustrious life as one of the prettiest undersea worlds he had ever seen. Cagayancillo which administers this region and its precinct including Tabbataha, is given special rights for the much-sought-after permit required of visitors to this protected area. We were promised that such permits would be made available to our team should we visit again.

That night I slept with dreams of this undersea paradise, with the most pristine water and fish life, and an island that neither Gauguin nor Brando has set foot on. Suddenly I saw a huge multi-deck cruise ship slowly rounding the corner of Cawili island. On the boat's balcony were tourists, hundreds of tourists, maybe even a thousand, in colorful Hawaiian shirts and shorts, shooting away with their cameras. Momentarily I woke up from this nightmare, and felt relieved that the rest of the world is still thousands of kilometers away. But for how long these places would remain isolated is anyone's guess. Maybe Ah Peng would have to sail even further to seek his safe haven.

La Rinna atoll / La Rinna 環礁

嘗試感受退休與我的憂鬱

FLIRTING WITH RETIREMENT AND MELANCHOLY

Inle Lake, Myanmar – January 8, 2017

嘗試感受退休與我的憂鬱　探險家的新年志願

我不習慣被侮辱，更別說在新年第一天了。

一月一日，二零一七年的元旦。我在銅鑼灣路邊的小店飽餐一頓蛇羹和臘腸飯之後，我決定試搭新營運的 *MTR*（香港地鐵）去辦公室。包括轉乘只有四站，而我這年紀的長者只要港幣兩元（等同 *0.25* 美元）。新路線剛在五天前的十二月二十八日開始營運，有一站離我們辦公室夠近，出站只需步行五分鐘。

雖然使用了長者優惠，但我從不認為自己的體力正在衰退像個接近退休的老人。事實上，我連想都沒想過退休，這念頭即使在潛意識裡也沒有。找接班人的計畫只是為了讓我可以有更多時間在野外探索，把募款、管理與讓組織逐漸壯大的事情丟給「接班人」。

我走進一列乾淨無瑕的新車廂，跟其他在新年第一天試乘新路線的人站在車門附近。畢竟我只搭兩站就該下車

FLIRTING WITH RETIREMENT AND MELANCHOLY

A New Year resolution for an explorer

I am not used to being insulted, let alone on the first day of the New Year.

It was January 1, New Year's Day of 2017. After a fine lunch in Causeway Bay at a street side shop with snake soup and Chinese sausage with rice, I decided to try the newly launched MTR (Hong Kong's metro subway) to our office. It was just four stops, including a change of train, and for a meager HK$2 (equivalent of US$0.25) for a senior of my age. The new line was just

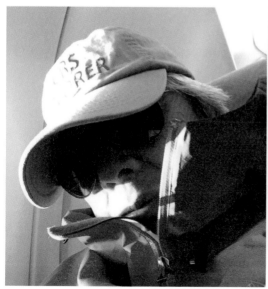 

HM with cap & shade / 戴帽子和墨鏡的黃效文   HM in the wild / 野外的黃效文

了。突然間有人拍我肩膀。我回頭看到一位小姐從座位起身讓位給我。「蛤？」我愣了一下。讓座給我？我比較習慣自己讓座給老人，還是她想跟我搭訕？不管怎麼樣我從來沒有想過自己是個老人！

我連忙婉拒轉身，回拒這份對老人的好意，這種善行在像香港這樣的大都會其實很少見了。但是我還是覺得被侮辱也覺得很尷尬。十幾年前我兩側頭髮開始變白，現在肯定越來越白了。我很少照鏡子，然而其他人對我的看法一定不同，尤其我的好友、支持者和同事。

我突然明白年輕這檔事必定只存在於我的腦子和心態裡，因為我沒有相符的身體、面孔或裝扮。到了辦公室，我趕緊戴上粉藍色的 CERS 帽子，戴上 Ray-Ban 墨鏡，希望下次搭車不會再有人讓座給我。隔天我嘗試同樣的路程，果然沒人讓座，頓時扳回了我的自尊。

為了讓自己平衡一點，我決定試試進入退休狀態，還有近乎沮喪的憂鬱，但只為期一週。畢竟，工作進展緊迫，我根本沒辦法憂鬱太久。要感覺憂鬱其實很容易，每當我無法閱讀或寫稿的時候，就會心情低落飽受挫折。

started five days ago on December 28 and one stop is efficiently close to our office, within five minute walk from the station.

While I take advantage of the discounted fare, I never quite consider my energy as that of someone approaching retirement and in decline. In fact, that thought has never been part of my notions, not even in my subconscious. Any plan of having a successor is only in order for me to spend more wild time in the field exploring, relegating operational matters of an organization in fundraising and managing our existing projects and growing staff to this "successor".

As I got into this spotlessly clean new train, I stood near the door among others trying out this new route on the first day of the New Year. After all, it was only two more stops to where I was supposed to get off. Suddenly someone tapped me on the shoulder. I looked around and a young lady had just risen from the end seat and gestured for me to sit down. "Huh?" I thought to myself momentarily. Me offered a seat? I am more used to myself offering a seat to elders, to ladies, or she's trying to pick me up, but never to being thought of as an old man!

I quickly declined and turned away, refusing this offer of courtesy for the elders, an act of kindness which is gradually disappearing in metro cities like Hong Kong. But in my mind I felt both insulted and embarrassed. My hair

BBQ along riverbank / 在河岸上烤肉
Breakfast on deck / 甲板上的早餐

had turned silver on the sides over a decade ago, and now they must be grey-ing. But I rarely if ever bother to look at myself in the mirror. Others must look at me differently however. Not least my close friends, supporters and associates.

I suddenly realized that the youth must be in my heart and mind only, and I don't have the body, face, or cosmetics to match. At the office, I quickly added a baby blue color CERS cap, donned my Ray-Ban shades, and hoped that no seat would be offered on my next ride. Indeed when I tried the same ride the next day, I redeemed my esteem and no seat was offered.

To offer myself some balance, I decided to try going into retirement, as well as melancholy margin on depression, but only for a week. After all, work in progress is pressing, and I cannot afford to be depressed for too long. The latter part is easy. Whenever I don't get to read or write, I get depressed and frustrated.

But lately, I have realized that my energy level has shifted during the day, though not in the month or year. I start each morning like a young man, not much different from days when I was in my prime, lively and energetic. I would even make plans for the evening, including after dinner. By noon and after lunch, my energy would go into decline and all my ambitions for the day would gradually dissipate, and plans for the evening would be canceled. By

但是最近又發現，我的體力會在一天中變化，而不是一個月或一年。我每天早上醒來像個年輕人，跟我年輕力壯時期沒什麼兩樣，活力飽滿。我甚至會安排晚上的計畫，甚至還安排晚餐以後的事。但是到中午吃過午飯後，我的體力開始衰退，規劃滿檔的一天到了下午開始走樣，晚上安排的活動也隨之被取消。到了晚飯時間，有些日子我會累到吃不完一餐，寧可直接去休息。我一輩子都習慣閱讀到我睡著，但是現在視力逐漸衰退，也沒有辦法再這樣做了。晚上的社交活動變得稀少。無可否認，年紀趕上我了。

這個新年，很幸運地我在一月三日跟幾位好友一起從香港出發去緬甸。午後不久，我們上了 *HM Explorer* 航行在伊洛瓦底江。對，沒有工作在身搭乘我們的探險船遊河的確是奢侈的事。這趟沒有科學家或攝影師隨行。*106* 呎的船搭載九位船員與工作人員，一趟單純的巡航。船上提供豐盛的三餐外，還有每天下午 *happy hour* 的飲料和點心。當中還有一次，在河邊的樹蔭下烤肉。新鮮果汁做的冰棒是大家的最愛，很享受的退休滋味啊！

這樣的生活，很快地又出現另一種滋味——沮喪。在我們抵達茵萊湖的項目點後，這感覺縈繞著許多天。

HM with Karl and Jeep / HM 與卡爾和吉普車合影

dinner time, there were days when I would struggle to finish the meal, prefer-
ring to simply relax to wind up the day. My deteriorating eyes also prevented
me from my life-long habit of reading myself to sleep. Social life in the evening
is becoming a rare event. Age is catching up, there is no denying.

For this New Year, fortunately, I left Hong Kong on January 3, heading with a
few good friends to Myanmar. By early afternoon, we were on board the HM
Explorer sailing up the Irrawaddy River. Yes, a river cruise on our exploration
vessel is a luxury when there is no work on our agenda. None of our scientists
or filmmakers is along. This is a straight cruise on a 106-foot boat with nine
in the crew and staff. Three sumptuous meals are served onboard; breakfast,

天然質樸的茵萊湖現在已經被觀光客和長艇淹沒，變成了度假勝地。看到我們最愛的緬甸貓躺在陽光下似乎對我也起了催眠作用。開著起步很慢的一九四五年 *Willys* 吉普車兜風，彷彿讓我進入了生活悠閒、時間很多的年代。

元旦日被「侮辱」的記憶未消，我想了一下或許這就是「低落」應有的樣子；睡覺，吃，再吃，然後睡覺。我整週感覺像個懶骨頭。

今天，新年過後一星期，我在清晨四點半起床，但整個上午還是什麼都不想做。午餐過後我午睡了一個多小時。終於，我在下午三點過後醒來，並逐漸振作起來，寫了第一封與工作有關的 *email* 給教授朋友，計畫未來的工作。我知道不能再沉溺於這個「低落」裡，還有工作在等著，而

President with Burmese cat / 總統抱著緬甸貓

lunch, and dinner, as well as happy hour with drinks and snacks every after-noon. On one occasion, we have a BBQ set up under the shade of a tree by the riverbank. As party favors, we even have icicles made from fresh juice, a taste of decadent retirement!

With such a life, soon another taste manifest itself - depression. It lingered on for the next few days as our group moved to our other project site at Inle Lake. Here, the fine life over a pristine lake, now flooded with tourists on long boats, provides a setting of a vacation mecca. Seeing our beloved Burmese Cats lying in the sun seems hypnotic for me as well. Taking a drive in a slow-start Willys Jeep of 1945 vintage brings me back to an age when life was slow and time was long.

With lingering thoughts about the "insult" I received on New Year's Day, I thought for a while perhaps this is what "depression" is supposed to be; sleep, eat, more eating, then sleep. I have felt like a couch potato for the entire week. Today, a week after the New Year, I pulled myself up at 4:30am but again didn't feel like doing anything the entire morning. I took over an hour nap right after lunch. Finally, I woke up after 3pm and got back into shape gradu-ally, writing my first work email to a professor friend to plan for work ahead. I know I cannot indulge in this "depression" any longer as work is waiting, and such "work" is what I enjoy most of all in my adult life and career.

這些「工作」是我成年就業後最喜愛的事。

突然我感覺活了過來，為明天作計劃，擠出半天時間去買補給品，為我們在菲律賓巴拉望的新項目買最好的蚊帳。開車到附近鎮上來回要四小時，但我在一個下午就輕鬆完成了。

至於早上，或許我該去探視我們的冠軍緬甸貓，芭比，牠在仰光貓展得到最高榮譽獎。雖然出身高貴，芭比還是有辦法溜出我們的緬甸貓保護區然後懷了孕回來。她生了三隻混種小貓，牠們是我看過最可愛的三隻花貓了。我們項目的夥伴 *Misuu* 嚇壞了不知該怎麼告訴我。但是我的好友，奧地利大公卡爾 · 馮 · 哈布斯堡在十一月跟我造訪緬甸貓咖啡店時，這事還是說出來了。卡爾靜靜聽著點頭表示讚許。同月稍早緬甸總統也到這裡參觀緬甸貓保護項目，似乎證實了這裡一切沒問題。

為了彌補過去的一週，今天早上我必須去看看我們的竹子工作室，跟我們支持的工匠夫婦討論。我帶了些在台灣竹山買的竹子玩具給他們參考，都是些簡單但很傳統的玩具，希望能在緬甸這裡複製，我相信這產業還有機會獲得新生命。手上的工作實在多到無法退

Suddenly I feel alive again, making plans for tomorrow, squeezing in a half day trip to buy supplies, the best mosquito nets, for our new project in Palawan in the Philippines. The drive to the nearby town is four hours roundtrip. That can easily be fitted into one afternoon.

For the morning, perhaps I should visit our champion Burmese cat Barbie which took top honor at the Cat Show in Yangon. Despite her royal accolade, Barbie somehow managed to sneak out of our Burmese Cat Sanctuary and came home pregnant. She gave birth to three bastards. They are the loveliest Calico cats I have ever set eyes on. Our project partner Misuu was horrified and did not know how to tell me the news. But it was told appropriately when my dear friend Karl von Habsburg, the Archduke of Austria, visited the Burmese Cat Café with me in November. Karl listened quietly and nodded in approval. A visit to the Burmese Cat Sanctuary by the President of Myanmar earlier in the month seems to validate that everything is quite alright.

To make up for a lost week, I must also visit our Bamboo Studio this morning and discuss with the craftsman couple whom we support. I have brought to them some bamboo toys I picked up at the Bamboo Mountain (Ju Shan) in Taiwan. Such simple but traditional toys, replicated here in Myanmar, should have a new lease on life. There is simply way too much work at hand to sink into retirement, let alone a depressed retirement.

休，更別提憂鬱的退休了。

茵萊湖中心周圍的步道伴隨著蓮花池，當我在之間遊走時心裡推敲著大片枯葉和蓮蓬之中少數幾朵遲開的花的謎題。從一九三二年起，我們的朋友 Nang 和她的家族就在此地經營傳統蓮絲編織品工作室，現在傳到第三代了。

連知名義大利高級織品商 Loro Piana 都從此地的蓮花絲找到靈感。但他們如果觀察蓮花的生態，或許會不解，蓮花是怎麼變成蓮蓬的？一旦遇到藍月，又是如何從蓮葉中竄出一個洞冒出頭來曬太陽的？那些洞比花或蓮蓬小得多。那些只看得見蓮花最終呈現的美貌或利益的人，可能永遠也想不通吧。或許該是學習坐在蓮花上的佛祖去尋找心靈解答的時候了。唵嘛呢叭咪吽。

Lotus pod protruding from leaf / 從葉子伸出來的蓮蓬

As I walk our long board walk over the lotus pond surrounding our modest center here at Inle Lake, I ponder in my mind the paradox of the few late blooming lotus blossom among a sea of withering leafs and lotus pods. Here is where our friend Nang and her family have maintained a traditional lotus silk weaving boutique workshop for three generations, since 1932.

Even Loro Piana, the famed Italian house of fine fabric, found inspiration here when they discovered the lotus silk. But if they were to observe the lotus life cycle, they may find a riddle. How does a lotus flower, later becoming a pod, once in a blue moon, penetrate a hole in a lotus leaf to rise above the surroundings to reach the sun? And the hole is much smaller than the ultimate flower or pod. Those who only see the resulting beauty, or the profit, from a lotus would never be able to figure it out. Perhaps it is time to seek a spiritual answer from the seated Buddha on a lotus. Om Mani Padme Hum.

Lotus in bloom / 盛開的蓮花

Lotus attracting bees / 蓮花引來蜜蜂

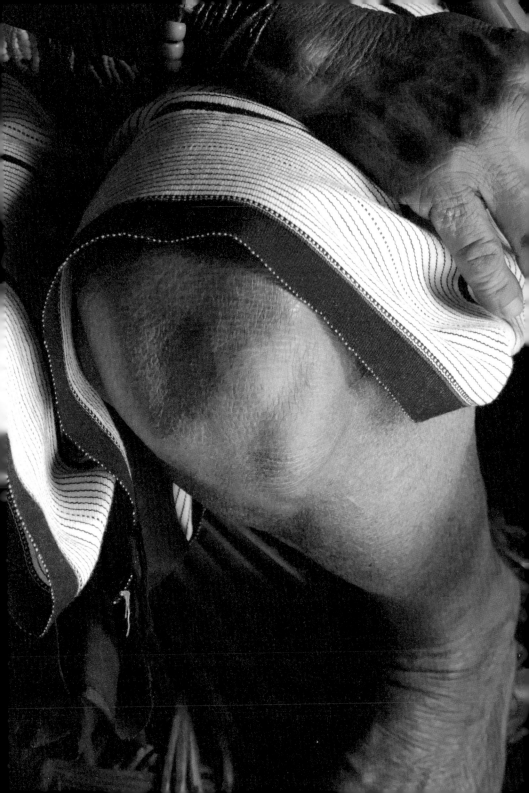

犀鳥之邦不再

HORNBILL STATE
NO MORE

Kanpetlet, Chin State, Myanmar – January 19, 2017

犀鳥之邦不再

「嗷啊嗚！」泰山一邊吼叫著一邊從在一棵樹盪到另一棵，抓住一根又一根藤蔓，像隻猴子穿越過叢林。但他那個出名的、已經被註冊成商標的叫聲，有可能是因為抓到長滿刺的藤蔓而發出的痛苦哀號。我們的欽邦嚮導湯瑪斯帶我看一棵年輕的籐蔓植物，大約十呎高，主幹上面佈滿了尖刺。

在南亞與東南亞，鞭刑被視為一種傳統刑罰，即便到今天也是。香港長大的我，還記得跟家裡的幫佣去傳統市場時看到有人在賣藤條。父母會用來處罰小孩，在當年這被視為最佳的管教工具。我和我的姊妹們都曾經被這種藤條管教過。

在我童年時代的學校教育中，用藤條管教也是被認為可接受的體罰。但在今日的「現代」社會，老師已不再被允許對學生施加任何體罰。時代變遷，或許有一天學生反過來傷害老師也會沒事。就在一年前，香港大學的學生示威中就發生了這種事。

HORNBILL STATE NO MORE

"Yaoooo-ahwooo-ahwoo!" Tarzan calls out while swinging from one tree to another, catching one liana after another, like a monkey through the jungle. But his yell, now registered as a trade mark, may well be a cry of pain, from catching the wrong vine, with a hand full of thorns. Thomas, our Chin guide, showed me a young rattan cane plant, about ten feet tall with its viney trunk covered with sharp thorns.

In South and Southeast Asia, caning is considered a traditional penal code even today. As a child growing up in Hong Kong, I remember going to the wet market with our maids where I would see canes for sale. Parents would use them to reprimand their children and it was then reckoned as the best tool for

Thomas with cane plant / 湯瑪斯與藤蔓　　Thorn of cane / 藤蔓的刺

「看到那些死掉的藤蔓從高大的樹上垂下來沒有？那就是藤條。本地人爬不到樹梢所以只能砍長得較低的分枝，因為它可以用來編出很好的籃子，」湯瑪斯指著一棵樹說。即使切得很薄，藤莖仍然很堅韌與有彈性，做成籃子可以用很多年。我們拜訪了做籃子的工匠 U Aung Kwee，但他透露現在藤條太難找，原料太貴了，所以他現在只用竹子編織。

如果藤上的刺摸起來很痛，那傳統欽邦婦女在臉部的刺青一定是更加痛苦。通常是由母親親自動手，將少女的臉刺滿部落圖騰，順序是先用藤刺在臉上戳滿小小的孔，然後再注入木炭和豆葉做成的靛藍墨汁到皮膚裡。「得要四、五個人壓住正在紋臉的少女，能忍痛的人可以在兩天內完成，但那些不能忍痛的人有可能會花上兩年的時間，每個月在臉上添加一點刺青。最痛的部分是眼皮上的刺青……」湯瑪斯向我透露紋面的秘密。

雖然紋面從一九六零年就被政府廢止，但是在偏遠部落仍然有人會偷偷地做這件事。我見過不到五十歲，或更年輕的婦女，仍有紋面刺青臉。當然了，所有老婦人，或至少「高雅」的老婦，都會必需有紋面刺青。

湯瑪斯三十三歲，在印度讀過四年書，所以英語流利。

disciplining. I, as well as my sisters, have all been recipients of such punishing discipline.

At school, caning was also considered acceptable in my childhood days. But in today's "modern" societies, teachers are no longer allowed to inflict the slightest bodily pain to students. In time, perhaps students may get away with incurring harm to teachers instead. That was exactly what happened during a student demonstration at Hong Kong University a year ago.

"You see those dead vines hanging down from a tall tree? That's cane. The locals cannot get to the top so they chop off the lower branches, as it can be used to weave the best baskets," said Thomas while pointing up a tree. Even when cut into fine thin pieces, rattan cane is strong and resilient, lasting many years when made into baskets. We visited a basket maker, U Aung Kwee, but he revealed that cane is too hard to find now and too expensive to purchase for basket making these days. Instead he weaves only from bamboo.

If the thorns of the cane hurt, the application of facial tattoo to a traditional Chin woman can be even more painful. A young girl would have her face fully tattooed with tribal markings, usually by her mother, using cane thorns to poke the face and injecting into the skin an indigo ink derived from charcoal and bean leaf. "With four to five persons holding down the young lady, those who can take pain can have it done within two days. But for those who can-

他已婚有兩個小孩；一個剛開始上學。「我是基督徒，但以前的欽邦人是泛靈論或薩滿教徒。現今大多數南部的欽邦人是佛教徒，而住北邊的主要是基督徒，」湯瑪斯告訴我。「然而，在南部的甘貝萊鎮，我們一共有十一座不同教派的教堂，」他補充說。唱歌是基督徒訓練的一部分，現在湯瑪斯在閒暇時間會擔任樂團的主吉他手。

這天是星期三，晚飯過後我聽見遠方傳來某種模糊的唱詩聲。「這是上教堂的人在唱歌。他們在週三晚上和週日在教會聚會，」湯瑪斯向我說明。「我過世的叔叔娶了個德國人，她用字母為我們欽邦人發明了書寫的欽

Tattoo lady / 紋面女士

not withstand pain would take a couple years, adding a bit of tattoo to the face each month. The most painful being tattooing to the eyelid," Thomas revealed to me the secrets of the practice.

Though face tattoo has been abolished by the government since 1960, remote villages still conduct it secretly. I have seen women below age 50, and younger, still bearing face tattoo. And of course, all older ladies, or at least "elegant" old ladies, would sport face tattoo.

Thomas, at 33 years old, had spent four years studying in India, thus is fluent in English. He is married and with two children; one just started school. "I am a Christian, but formerly Chin people are animists and shamanists.

Hunter's wife with tattoo / 有紋面的獵人之妻

邦文。因此,她獲得了博士學位。現在我的嬸嬸已經八十幾歲了,住在仰光。」湯瑪斯又說。我問了她的地址,告訴湯瑪斯,How Man 博士下次去仰光時,一定會去探望緬甸名字叫 Daw Helga So 的 Hard Man 博士。

甘貝萊是個接近山脊的欽族高地小社區,全國將近五十萬的欽族人有一部份是住在這裡。許多家庭,像湯瑪斯的父母,最近才搬來這裡。以湯瑪斯來說,他是四歲時來的,跟父母從老家村莊往南方走了三天才落腳這裡。他們搬來是為了讓小孩受更好的教育。在大多數村莊,只有小學而已;為了上初中,許多欽族家庭在最近十幾二十年紛紛搬來這裡。

Shwe Htain 的家人七年前也是為了相同理由搬來此地。以前在老家,他們可以從印度買棉花,染成他們想要的顏色,然後編織成很漂亮的欽族毯子。但是現在,他們已經沒有辦法這樣做了,Shwe Htain 說她自從搬到山上的甘貝萊之後連一顆棉花子都沒見過。她的客廳櫥櫃裝了一堆折疊整齊的彩色毯子,都是從老家帶來的。還有兩疊白底襯著紅色條紋。

「一條大約八乘六呎的毯子多少錢?」Shwe Htain 回答說四萬緬元,大約是三十美元。 我迅速地選了六條各

Today most Chin people in the southern part of the State are Buddhists whereas those living to the north are mainly Christians," Thomas revealed to me. "Nonetheless, here in the town of Kanpetlet in the south, we have 11 churches of various denominations in all," he added. Singing is part of his Christian training, and today Thomas plays lead guitar and perform with a band during his spare time.

It was a Wednesday and in the evening after dinner I could hear the chanting of some unintelligible hymns from a distance. "These are the church goers singing. They get together on Wednesday evening and Sunday for church services," Thomas explained to me. "My late uncle married a German lady who invented our Chin writing, using alphabets. For that, she received a doctorate. Now my auntie still lives in Yangon though she is over 80 years of age," Thomas added. I got her address and told Thomas that Dr. How Man would certainly look up Dr. Hard Man, a.k.a. Daw Helga So in Burmese, when I next visit Yangon.

Kanpetlet is a small Chin community high up near the mountain ridge, part of almost half a million Chin people in the entire country. Many families, like Thomas' parents, moved here only recently. For Thomas, he came when he was four years old, hiking with his parents for three days from the former village to the south. They moved such that their children could receive better education. In most villages, there are only primary schools. In order to attend

種顏色的毯子。但是突然間價格漲了 50%，一條毯子變成了六萬緬元。我心想她也太貪婪投機了。

幾回合議價之後，才知道原來是她根本不想割愛，因為他們沒有辦法再做毯子了。毯子被視為傳家之寶，也是一種財富展示，越多越好，總不能把錢拿出來展示吧。對欽族來說，牲口和毯子是用來衡量財富的標準，她總共擁有超過四十幾條的毯子。我於是耐心地交涉懇求，終於以每條四萬五千緬元成交了六條，這些都是 CERS 重要的收藏。我們離開之前，我還買了個藤編的刀鞘，跟一顆舊犀鳥頭。

Chin blankets / 欽族毛毯

secondary school, many Chin families moved here within the last ten to twenty years.

Shwe Htain's family moved here seven years ago for the same reason. From their previous home, they could buy cotton from India, dye it to their colors of choice, and weave the very lovely Chin blankets. Today, they can no longer make the same, and Shwe Htain said she hadn't even seen a single cotton seed since arriving in Kanpatlet, high up in the mountain. Her living room cabinet was filled with stacks of colorful blankets, nicely folded, that she brought from her old home. There were also two stacks of white ones with red stripe designs.

I asked how much for a blanket, each measuring roughly eight feet by six feet. Shwe Htain said 40,000 Kyats, or the equivalent of $30USD. I quickly picked out six blankets of various colors and offered to pay her. Suddenly the prices went up 50% to 60,000 Kyats. I thought she was most greedy and speculating on prices.

After rounds of negotiation, it turned out that she really did not want to part with her blankets at all, as they could no longer make them. They are considered heirlooms, and it is a demonstration of wealth in the family to have as many blankets as possible, and in full sight. Money cannot be shown, but livestock and blankets are the measure of wealth in Chin families. As her stacks

湯瑪斯告訴我過去的習俗是如果有人殺豬跟社區分享，就會收到不同家庭回送的 5 條毯子。若是宰牛，就會收到 15 條毯子以示表揚。但是現在這種大方分享和回禮的傳統習俗已經完全消失了。

我們住在一家新開張的山區客棧，有六間小屋，是 *Sorlong* 村的社區公營企業。原來我們是客棧的第一批顧客，因此得到 VIP 級的禮遇。湯瑪斯兼任這裡的經理與嚮導。我問湯瑪斯，當嚮導這麼多年，有沒有看過中國觀光客來欽邦。他豎起一根手指，然後指向我。晚上我們圍著溫暖的營火，欣賞附近村民為我們準備的節目，傳統樂團演奏的音樂與舞蹈。

隔天，湯瑪斯帶我們進村裡去拜訪一位老婦，*Daw Bwe Htang*，滿臉紋面的七十歲老人。她坐在凳子上抽著一根很大的水煙。長管上都是銅環，末端是個葫蘆。她每抽一口就發出冒泡的水聲。接著她拿出一支長竹笛，不發一語，把笛子湊到鼻子上吹了起來。我三十多年前聽過海南的黎族人演奏過鼻笛，但這支笛子響亮多了，或許因為這位七旬老嫗很賣力吹。過了一會兒，她站了起來一面演奏一面繞著小圈跳舞。

幾分鐘後，吹完兩曲，*Bwe Htang* 坐到她的凳子上拿起

must have over forty blankets in total, I patiently negotiated and begged, and finally left with half a dozen blankets at 45,000 Kyats each, an important collection for CERS. Before we parted, I even acquired a knife sheath woven from cane, as well as an old hornbill head.

Thomas told me that it was customary in the past that if someone killed a pig to share with the community, he would be given five blankets by different families. If a cow was slaughtered, 15 blankets would be received as honor. But today such sharing and traditional reciprocation of generosity has all been lost.

We stayed at a newly opened mountain lodge with six cottages which was set up as a community social enterprise of Sorlong Village. It turned out we were the very first customers of the lodge and were given VIP treatment. Thomas is both the manager and the guide. I asked Thomas whether, in all his years of guiding, he had seen any Chinese visitor to the Chin region. He put up one finger, and then lowered his finger to point at me. In the evening the nearby villagers treated us to music by a traditional orchestra and dancing around a very warm bon fire.

On the second day, Thomas took us into the village to visit an old lady, Daw Bwe Htang, 70 years old with full face tattoo. She was sitting on a stool and smoking a gigantic water pipe. It had brass rings all around the long

掛在脖子上的竹製口簧琴開始演奏，旋律非常迷人。接著，她換了另一支音調稍微不同的口簧琴繼續演奏。湯瑪斯說這種音樂大致失傳了，在他們這裡老婦是唯一僅存的演奏者了，若她過世後，這一切就真的失傳了。

我再度想起這種獨特文化必須被重視與記錄，而且要越快越好。我知道我們攝影師不久後就會來記錄這位國寶女士。我也想到保存與挽救這些在地文化應該是一個尋求身分認同的國家應該考量的。雇用兩個年輕欽族女子向 Daw Bwe Htang 學習能有多困難？在法國與日本這種國家，對文化保存與身懷絕技的人備受尊崇，會被當作人間國寶受到尊敬與重視。Daw Bwe Htang 的演奏絕對夠格在世界上任何聲望很高的的表演廳登台。

作為道別禮物，老婦選了兩支口簧琴中較好的一支送我們當紀念品。我非常感激心裡暗自承諾一定會很快回來記錄她的技藝和她的故事。她的口簧琴曲子靈感來自犀鳥，是欽邦的邦鳥。他們說口簧琴是模仿這種大鳥振翅的聲音，犀鳥振翅時發出的聲音可以傳的很遠，有人說甚至可達一公里！

但是就像 Daw Bwe Htang 演奏的曲子，欽邦人奉為部落

spout arriving at a gourd at the end. The bubbling noise of water sounded
with her every puff. Next she brought out a long bamboo flute. Without
saying a word, she put the flute to her nose and began playing. I had heard
nose flutes played by the Hainan Li people over 30 years ago, but this flute

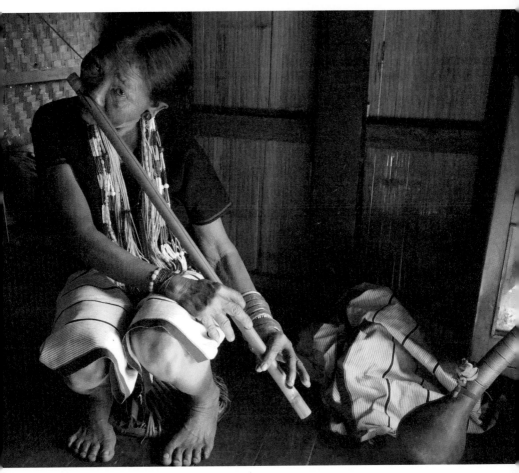

Playing nose-flute / 吹鼻笛

Playing Jew's Harp / 演奏口簧琴

象徵的犀鳥也變得越來越稀少。湯瑪斯說他們已經十幾
年沒在這裡見過犀鳥了，犀鳥們幾乎已被捕獵殆盡。
附近一間咖啡店裡，竹屏上畫著大犀鳥，似乎紀念著
這消失的邦鳥。

回到客棧，睡前百感交集，想著欽邦之美和他們消失中
的文化。半夜，我被雞啼聲吵醒，不久就傳來遠處各村
落呼應的雞啼聲。我看看錶，剛過凌晨兩點。過了兩
分鐘牠們的叫聲很快平息下來，我也逐漸睡去。畢竟，
公雞太早叫了，還有兩星期才是雞年呢。

*was much louder, due perhaps to the effort this 70-years-old used blowing
into it. After a moment, she stood up and started a small circular dance
without ever stopping the music.*

*A few minutes later, after two songs, Bwe Htang sat down on her stool and
took up a bamboo Jew's Harp hanging around her neck and started playing.
The rhythm was very charming. Next, she changed to another Jew's Harp
with a slightly different tone and continued. Thomas said such music had
largely disappeared and in their area this lady was the only performer remaining. It would naturally die with her passing.*

*It brought to mind once again that such unique culture must be valued and re-
corded, as soon as possible. In my mind, I knew our filmmaker would soon be
here to document this treasure lady. It also crossed my mind that the preservation and saving of these indigenous cultures should be the concern of a country seeking its own identity and integrity. How difficult would it be to pay for
a couple young Chin ladies to learn from Daw Bwe Htang? In countries like
France and Japan, cultural preservation and persons with such talent would
be put on a pedestal, revered and valued as a living national treasure. Daw
Bwe Htang's rendition could have graced any stage at the most prestigious
performing halls of the world.*

As a parting present, the old lady chose the better of her two Jew's Harps and

太陽不久就會升起。或許欽族也會復興，他們的年輕世代將會繼承 *Daw Bwe Htang* 的衣缽。希望這不只是另一場夢！

Traditional Chin house / 傳統欽族房屋

presented it to us as a souvenir. I could not thank her enough, but promised in my heart that we would soon return to record her art and her story. Her song on the Harp was inspired by the Hornbill, the State Bird of Chin State. I was told that it imitated the flapping sound of the huge bird, which in life can be heard from a great distance, some say up to one kilometer!

But like Daw Bwe Htang's passing songs, the Hornbills that the Chin people hold as symbol of their tribe are becoming more and more scarce. Thomas said that they haven't seen any in their region for over ten years now. They've simply been hunted out. In a nearby café, a huge painted Hornbill on a bamboo screen stood to eulogize the passing of a stately bird.

Back at the community lodge, I went to sleep with mixed thoughts about the beauty of the Chin and their eclipsing culture. In the middle of the night, I was awakened by a rooster's call, soon followed by a chorus of answering calls from all around the distant villages. I looked at my watch and it was barely past 2am. Their calls soon died after a couple minutes and I gradually fell back to sleep. After all, the roosters had called prematurely, as the Year of the Chicken was still two weeks away.

The sun would soon rise. Perhaps the Chin also will rise again, and their young generation will take up from where Daw Bwe Htang left off. Hopefully it is not just another dream!

巴塔克山區部落

BATAK HILL TRIBE – LESS THAN 300 REMAINING

Palawan, Philippines – February 3, 2017

巴塔克山區部落——剩下不到 300 人

「我跳舞，但不在火上，」我們走向第一間巴塔克屋時，安娜莉札開玩笑說。顯然先前的訪客，曾經粗魯地冒犯族人，可能失禮地要求她跳舞，在火上跳。人們認為原住民都很異國也野蠻。難怪因為這種刻板印象，讓巴塔克族漸漸往叢林的深處退去。

我們的嚮導阿迪來自百大洞穴，一個社區型的觀光企業，那是 CERS 正在參與的計畫之一。阿迪從小就會來 Kayasan 村玩，他會說巴塔克語，村子裡有一些人，跟徒步約半天遠的巴塔克人通婚。「二十年前，這個村子有好多房子，是個真正的社區，」阿迪說。「但現在只有大概十棟房子，大多數的人搬到山裡去，半天到一天路程那樣遠的地方」他補充說。

巴塔克人是十分害羞並且與世隔絕的民族。一旦外人開始上門，他們會選擇搬走。在過去，靠採集森林物資生存的巴塔克人會狩獵、墾地和火耕，與鄰近部落只有很少的接觸。他們聲稱如果道路開到他們的居住領域，他

BATAK HILL TRIBE – LESS THAN 300 REMAINING

"I dance, but not on fire," cracked Annaliza as we walked up toward the first Batak house. Obviously previous visitors, perhaps crude and intrusive ones, may have insensitively asked for her to dance, and preferably over fire. Such may be the common conception that natives are exotic and savages. No wonder with such stereotype image, the Batak are receding deeper and deeper into the jungle.

Our guide Ady from the 100 Caves community-based tourism venture, which CERS has been assisting, has been here in Kayasan village many times since a child. He speaks Batak and some of those in his village, maybe half-day hike away, have intermarried with the Batak. "Twenty years ago, this village has so many houses, a real community," said Ady. "But today only about ten houses scattered around as most have moved further into the mountains, another half day to one day distance away," he added.

The Batak are very shy and secluded people. Once outside people began arriving, they choose to move away. In the past, the Batak, who subsist on collecting forest products, hunting and slash and burn farming, only have marginal

們就會搬進叢林的更深處。

Google 搜尋巴拉望的巴塔克人，出現的圖像會顯示這些「異國」男女裸露著上身。這些人類學家在一九六零到七零年代分享的影像吸引了好奇地探險者與觀光客前來，希望可以看到人口剩餘不到三百的巴塔克族。

我自己的好奇心則有多重面向。自從 CERS 在注入蘇祿海的河口附近設立基地之後，我們就急欲探索 Maoyon 河上游。我向來對河流的源頭很著迷。Maoyon 河由西向東橫跨整個巴拉望島，美麗的石灰岩山──克麗歐派特拉山的山腳下，蘊藏著一條地底下的河流，這裡也是一個世界遺產的位置。

CERS 團隊希望能探索這條河流，一條蜿蜒整個巴拉望，有效地將它切成兩半的整條河流。上游穿過巴塔克人的區域，絕佳的自然與文化的結合，再適合我們不過了。或許我們有機會還可以作出一點貢獻呢。

就在兩個月前，畢尉林博士和 CERS 攝影師李伯達搭竹筏沿河漂流了 21 公里，而那三位船夫就是巴塔克人。他們搭造簡陋的竹筏駕著它通過急流，花了大約七小時抵達我們的基地。那是我們第一次跟巴塔克人接觸。但現在

contacts with neighboring tribes. They have threatened to move even deeper into jungle recesses if a road were ever to be built into their region of abode.

Google the Batak of Palawan and images will show these "exotic" people, both men and women, baring their upper body. And perhaps such images shared from the 1960s and 70s by anthropologists attracted the arrival of curious adventurers and tourists wishing to see the remnant of less than 300 of these Batak people.

My own curiosity is multi-faceted. We are eager to explore the upper reaches of the Maoyon River since CERS is setting up a base near its mouth where it enters into the Sulu Sea. Forever I have had a fascination with river sources. The Maoyon crosses the entire island of Palawan from west to east, starting

Batak people / 巴塔克人

我想要更進一步，從更上游的地方，或許再往上五公里。然後再多下一點功夫，我要去拜訪最近的巴塔克村落。畢竟，將來他們會是我漂流的船員、船長、大副和二副。

我要求在我抵達前建造一艘更大更好的竹筏。我們從百大洞穴開始進山，渡過大大小小的七條溪，來到第一座巴塔克村落。路況惡化時，我轉搭乘一台本地水牛拉的

On a Kara / 坐菲律賓水牛車

from the foothills of Mount Cleopatra, a most beautiful limestone mountain under which the Underground River, a World Heritage Site, is located.

Together with my team, we wanted to explore the entire length of this river, which meanders and effectively cuts Palawan into two halves. The upper section penetrates the region of the Batak people, a perfect combination for our work on both nature and culture. Maybe we can avail ourselves of opportunities to make some contributions.

Just two months ago, Dr Bleisch and CERS filmmaker Xavier floated down 21 kilometers of the river on a bamboo raft. It turned out the three rafters were Batak. They built the rickety raft and piloted it down the rapids, which took some seven hours to get to our base. That was our first contact with the Batak. But now I want to take it further and start rafting from higher up the river, perhaps another five kilometers upstream. And with a bit of extra effort, I will visit the closest Batak village. After all, they'll be my boatmen, Captain, First and Second mates.

I asked for a larger and better raft to be built before my arrival. We started by hiking up from 100 Caves, crossing seven streams large and small in getting to the first Batak village. When the going got tough, I moved on to riding in a native buffalo cart which carried my supplies, food, water, and tents. This off-road 4x4 which the locals called Karabao is more than a workhorse, pulling

牛車，載運我的補給品、糧食、飲水和帳篷。當地人稱作菲律賓水牛的這種野外四足驅動載具不只是駄獸，還能拉動沉重牛車爬上陡峭的泥濘路面。雖然路程顛簸，但是我們的興奮感彌補了肉體的不適。

我的車伕發明了一套簡單但有效的剎車系統，用繩子橫向綁在水牛的前腿後方，有效地阻止牠邁開大步。然後車伕會用雙腳往前或往後地踩踏綁著的繩索，前個動作會在下坡時限制牛的速度，若是把牛尾巴往前拉，就成了手剎車，施予一點疼痛讓牠走慢點。放開雙腳與雙手剎車，水牛就會用正常的步伐上坡或行走。

終於抵達 Maoyon 河之後，我的保時捷級竹筏已經準備好了，有一個陽春的桌子跟兩個長板椅，連頂篷都有。前甲板有某種剎車可以一腳踩住，避免撐筏前進時在竹子上滑倒。還有名符其實的三段變速排檔，因為船長身旁有三種不同長度的竹竿可選擇，要看河水深度決定出動哪根。

這個地點大約在河的兩條支流匯合處上游五公里，距離巴塔克人的 Kayasan 村還要走上一小時。我的團隊非常體恤我，因為從這裡無法行駛牛車；他們撐竿推竹筏逆流而上，為我保留我的腿力走最後一段路。憑著技巧和

the heavy cart up steep terrain on mud and dirt tracks. While the ride was bumpy, the excitement made up for the discomfort.

My coachman devised a simple but functional brake system, a rope tide sideways behind the front legs of the buffalo, thus effectively prohibiting its legs from taking big stride. This is applied by the driver using his two feet to push forward or backward on the attached rope. The former motion would restrict the buffalo's speed when going downhill, and there's a handbrake by pulling the buffalo's tail forward, hurting it enough to make it slow even further. Releasing both the foot and hand brakes would allow the buffalo to go uphill or take normal strides.

Applying handbrake / 使用手剎車

努力，他們克服了三處小急流，團隊的五個人甚至全部都跳下河幫忙推船，我夠老可以留在船上，我一邊開玩笑說萬一沉船我寧可跟竹筏共存亡。在這種地方，我的保時捷突然變成了福斯老爺金龜車。

最後我們抵達一處河彎，停下靠岸，從這裡走了半小時前往最近的巴塔克村子。我們先經過了一個塔格巴努亞部落，再穿過樹叢密布的小路通往山麓。有兩條小溪要渡過，但算是平緩輕鬆。

繞過一處轉彎後，我們看到第一間巴塔克房屋和安娜莉札，她用很妙的玩笑話迎接我們。她離婚之後改嫁，女兒麗莎十一歲，兒子是個圓頭胖小子，才兩歲。腰掛大鐮刀的安娜莉札看來像極了亞馬遜女戰士。她家離 *Kayasan* 村聚落還有一小段路，身為獨立勇敢的巴塔克女人，她把家蓋在村子的墓地旁邊。

靠她帶路，我們進入村子，幾公頃的面積散落著大約十棟房屋，中央有座破爛籃球場。大多數房子現在有波浪鐵皮屋頂，最大的建築物是老舊的 *Kayasan* 基督教堂，我聽說是韓國傳教團體捐贈的。傳教士們一定很高興看到他們的傳教和禱告有了成果，現在所有巴塔克人都穿上了衣服，跟卅年前大不相同。聽說不遵從新的衣著規

When I finally reached the Maoyon River, my Porsche of a bamboo raft stood waiting, with a make-shift table and two benches, even a canopy. It came with kind of a brake on the fore deck as a hold for one foot to avoid slipping on the bamboo while poling the raft forward. It also came with three-speed stick shift, literally, as there were three different lengths of bamboo poles on the side for the Captain to choose from, depending on the depth of the river.

The location was about five kilometres above the confluence of two tributaries of the river. The Batak village of Kayasan was still over an hour hike away. My crew decided to save me the difficult hike, as from here no ox cart can go; they would pole the raft upriver to preserve my legs for the last stretch. With skills and hard work, we negotiated three small rapids, at which points all five people in my party would jump off the raft and push the vessel through. I was senior enough to stay onboard, as I joked that I would prefer going down with our raft if it should sink. In such locations, my Porsche would suddenly become an old VW beetle.

Finally we reached a bend of the river where we moored, and from here we hiked for a half hour toward the nearest Batak village. First we passed through a small village of the Tagbanua tribe, then pushed through some thick bushes with a tiny footpath into the foothills. There were a couple small streams to cross, but the going was level and easy.

定的人都搬到叢林的更深處去了，要花上半天到一天的腳程才能到達。

我們參觀了幾棟房屋，這過程中無論我們在哪裡，村民們不分老幼都會很快地聚集過來。有棟小竹屋裡的婦人病得幾乎無法起床，但她給了我們兩個為聖誕節製作的竹編圓圈裡面崁著星星。我到訪期間村裡只見到兩三個男人，至於其他的男人，大約有三十人，全到山上採集樹脂去了。他們可能要一個半月才會回來。

當地人自古以來稱作 *Almaciga* 的菲律賓貝殼杉，高大但也瀕臨絕種。木材可燃，被各部落用作燃料。但它的樹脂，分成幾個等級，最高級是白色的，較次級的則是暗黃色，是很好的家具亮光漆，在法國、德國甚至日本都很受歡迎。還有人傳說法國人還用它來做香料。採收樹脂成為巴塔克人的經濟來源。然而他們辛辛苦苦收集來的樹脂，每公斤只能賺七披索，而在城市裡的中盤商可以賣到三倍以上的價錢。賣到海外市場，價錢還會再翻上幾倍。

同樣的森林也出產藤條，巴塔克人一樣會採來賣。他們會採集的第三樣東西是品質非常好的野蜂蜜。據說巴塔克人生活方式從自給自足改變為採集物資賣到市場，換

And as we rounded a bend, we encountered the first Batak hut and Annaliza, who greeted us with her wise crack. She was divorced and now remarried. Her daughter Liza is 11 years old and the son, a round-headed chubby boy, is 2. Annaliza looked every bit an Amazon with her long machete by her waist. Her house is a short walk from the main village of Kayasan. An independent and brave Batak woman, she set up her home next to the village cemetery.

With her leading, we went into the village, a scattering of perhaps ten houses spread out on the periphery of a plot maybe a few hectares in area, with a run-down basketball court in the center. Most houses now have a corrugated metal roof, the biggest building being the rundown Kayasan Christian Church, donated by a Korean missionary group I was told. The missionaries must be pleased to see that their preaching and prayers are seeing fruition as all Batak people are clothed today, a far cry from 30 years ago. Those who did not adopt the new dress code I heard had moved further into the jungle, a half day to full day hike away.

We visited a few houses. Wherever we were, soon the rest of the villagers gathered, adults and children. One woman in a tiny bamboo house was so sick she could hardly get up. But she gave us two woven bamboo stars in a circular ring she had made for Christmas. There was only two to three men in the village during my visit. The rest of them, maybe up to 30, were up in the hills gathering copal. It may take up to a month and a half before they return.

取一些錢可以買米、衣服和其他小東西，這樣的改變減少了他們花在採集食物與狩獵的時間精力。實質上，這打亂了他們先前的飲食平衡。他們必須比以前更努力工作，因此減少他們的熱量攝取，結果他們的生育率下降而夭折率升高，他們的健康變差和人口減少，這真是文明化的一大反諷。

我初次造訪巴塔克人時間很短，因為我們還得走回竹筏，在河邊紮營過夜。那天晚上，我坐在營火邊看著螢火蟲伴隨星辰與銀河共舞。另一種蟲也在跳舞。蠓（Niknik）是一種吸血的沙蟎，正被我招待吃大餐。我知道我們會再回來，或許還會帶幾位學者來觀察並構想我們可以為這個地區做些什麼。畢竟，這個巴塔克村落像個血管連接 Maoyon 河，也連接我們在河口的新基地。

Batak woman / 巴塔克婦女

The locals call it Almaciga, from the ancient, tall and endangered Agathis Philippinensus tree. Its wood is flammable and used by the tribes for fire. But its resin, divided into the highest grade, which is white, and lower grades of yellow and dark, is highly prized as furniture varnish, sought by the French, German and even the Japanese. Stories also circulate that the French maybe using it for fragrance as well. Tapping the Almaciga has become a cash crop for the Batak. However each kilogram, collected through hard, tough work, only yields 7 peso for them, whereas in the city it would be worth three times as much for the middle men. By the time it reaches overseas market, it would cost multiples more.

The same forest would produce also rattan cane that the Batak would collect and sell to the market. A third item high on their collecting list is wild bee honey, and of very superior quality. It is said that by changing their lifestyle from subsistence to collecting for the market, the Batak are receiving some

Annaliza's boy / 安娜莉札的兒子   Batak mother & daughter / 巴塔克母女

隔天駕筏花了九個小時才回到我們的基地，有時通過急流，有時撐竿通過平緩的河段。最棒的是竹筏經過叢林樹蔭下，目睹一隻綠鸚鵡、兩隻猴子、三隻巴拉望犀鳥，還有五條蛇，這五條都掛在我們頭頂的樹枝上。

蛇為什麼總喜歡掛在河面上的樹枝呢？巴塔克人說，蛇俯瞰水面像照鏡子一樣，查看自己的大小，才知道可以吞下多大的獵物。我希望這是真的，那我就沒什麼好擔心，因為我的體重與身材日漸增加，已經大到

Poling downriver / 撐船往下游

cash to purchase rice, clothes and other small items, while reducing time and effort in food collecting and hunting. Thus in real returns, the new preoccupation has disrupted their former dietary balance. They have to work much harder than before, compromising their calorie intake, and as a result their reproduction rate has gone down while infant mortality went up, diminishing their health and numbers, an irony of going higher in the civilization scale.

My first visit with the Batak is necessary short as we had to hike back to our raft and spending the night camping by the river. That evening, I sat around our campfire watching the fireflies dancing with the stars and the Milky Way. Another type of flies was dancing too. Niknik, a kind of blood-sucking sand mites, were having a feast, compliment of yours truly. But I knew my team would return, perhaps even with a few more scholars to observe and devise what we may be able to do in this region. After all, the Batak village is connected through the Maoyon like a vein to our new base at the mouth of the River.

Rafting back to our base the next day took nine hours, at times through rapids, and at other times poling through flat stretches of the river. The best moments were when we rafted through some under cover of the jungle, sighting one green parrot, two monkeys, three Palawan Hornbills, and five snakes, the last of which were all seen overhead on trees as we went under cautiously.

蛇無法消受了！

Campsite by river / 河邊的營地

The Batak has a story about why snakes always like to stay on trees overhanging the river. The snake looks down at the river like a mirror to check its own size, so it knows how large a prey it can devour. I hope the story is true, as then I have little reason to worry, because with my gaining of weight and size, I am now too large to fit the snake's appetite!

最後的捕魚水獺

LAST OF THE FISHING OTTER

Hejiang, Sichuan – February 17, 2017

最後的捕魚水獺

我並不喜歡寫到「最後」的任何東西。那顯得很悲觀、負面，又沒建設性。但是最近我老是寫「最後」的什麼，無論關於無法逆轉的大自然變化，或更常見的，消失中的文化遺產。

而亞洲河獺這個例子，更橫跨了自然與文化這兩方面。水獺數量減少，一是因為人們為了取得牠們的皮毛，二是因為水獺逐漸喪失了天然的棲地，因此數量愈來愈少。就文化方面來說，馴化河獺捕魚的古老方式也已經逐漸消失。這裡的「逐漸」，其實是快轉的意思。

我初次發現漁民用水獺捕魚是在三十多年前，一九八五年為美國國家地理雜誌出征到長江探險期間。當時，我搭乘充氣橡皮艇船從重慶溯江航行。某天日出前，在合江縣赤水匯入長江的匯流處，我遇到五六艘夜間出去捕魚返家的小舢舨。每艘舢舨上都有一隻馴化過的水獺來幫助他們捕魚。

Hejiang, Sichuan – February 17, 2017

LAST OF THE FISHING OTTER

I don't like writing about the "last" of anything. It seems pessimistic, negative, and non-productive. But recently I have been always writing about the "last" of things, be it regarding an irreversible change with nature or, more often, eclipsing cultural heritage.

In the case of the Asiatic River Otter, it strides both nature and culture. On the one hand, the otters are becoming rarer and rarer, due in part to hunting of their fur as well as loss of habitat. On the other hand, the ancient culture of domesticating river otter to fish is becoming extinct. "Becoming" in fast-forward.

I first discovered fishermen using otters to fish during my National Geographic Yangtze expedition in 1985, over 30 years ago. At the time, I was sailing in our Zodiac inflatable boat upriver from Chongqing. One early morning just before sunrise, at the confluence of Qishui, a river joining the Yangtze at Hejiang, I encountered half a dozen small sampans returning home after a night of fishing. Each sampan had an otter, domesticated to help the fishermen in their catch.

隔天下午我們跟著他們出去捕魚拍攝他們工作的情
形。但在當時攝影機很原始，無法在昏暗光線或黑夜
中拍攝。當時我發誓一定還要再回來。

十幾年後，我真的回去了，在二零零六年回到長江邊的

We went out with them again the following afternoon and filmed them in action. But at the time, our videocam was primitive and unable to pick up activities in dim light or after dark. I vowed to return.

Otter fishing c.1985 / 約 1985 年水獺捕魚

合江，努力地尋找水獺漁民。我很失望連一個都找不到。但是後來在下游處，我們找到一戶人家還有一隻水獺能捕魚。一位父親和四個兒子以前分別各有自己的船和水獺，五個男丁共有五隻水獺。但是到了二零零六年，只剩次子王達明（音譯）還保留著最後一隻會捕魚的水獺。

如今又過了十年，我又回去拜訪，帶著我們的攝影師李伯達跟先進多的器材去紀錄這個古老行業的最後一幕。雖然王達明已經五十四歲，但仍舊活躍地捕魚，他的水獺還是十一年前的那「么哥」。但是時間所剩不多，耀哥已經十二歲了，不可能指望他一直捕魚下去，更別說永遠不死了。

「首先要買到水獺來訓練就是很困難的。其次，你得要有許可證，這就更是難上加難了」王達明說。「訓練算是輕鬆的部分。成年水獺比較容易訓練。給我三個月就能讓牠變成捕魚高手。」

「么哥學會最重要的一堂課是把前肢往後揮，這樣在網子裡潛水時，牠的爪子才不會被網子卡到，」達明又說。他下了個簡短的口令同時拍拍么哥的身體側邊。么哥立刻往後收起前肢，貼在身體兩側。現在，達明

Return I did, over ten years later, back to Hejiang by the Yangtze in 2006, and made a rigorous search for remains of the practice. I was disappointed that none, not even one such otter fisherman, could be found. Further downriver however, we found one family with a single otter still in action. The father and four sons used to each have their own boat and an otter, five otters to a family of five male members. But by 2006, only Wang Daming, the second of the siblings, managed to keep to the last otter.

Anther ten years on, I went back for a visit, this week, together with our filmmaker Xavier with much better equipment to record this finale of an age-old practice. Wang Daming, now 54 years of age, is still actively involved with fishing with the same otter, Yao Ge, from 11 years ago. But the clock is ticking. Yao Ge is 12 years old and cannot be expected to live, let alone fish, forever.

"First it is difficult to an find otter to buy and train. Secondly, you must get a permit, which is even more difficult to acquire," Daming said. "Training is the easy part. An adult otter is easier to train than a young one. Give me three months and I can have it fishing like a champion."

"One of the most important lessons was for Yao Ge to learn to swing his fore limbs backward, so when diving inside the net, his claws would not get caught by the net," Daming added. He gave a short command while patting the side

的雙胞胎兒子沒人願意接班，他們認為水獺漁夫的生活太辛苦了。

達明的哥哥達永六十歲，當我們夜晚隨達明出去捕魚時他划著第二艘船協助我們拍攝的工作。「水獺就像我們的家人一樣，我的水獺死掉時，我將牠厚葬還做了墳墓，」他回憶說。但是如同其他人，他再也沒辦法找到可以替代的水獺了。

達明告訴我水獺非常寶貴。過去人們獵捕水獺為了取牠們優質的皮毛。中國漁民在幾百年前成功地馴化牠們來捕魚。連馬可波羅都在他的遊記中提到這種捕魚法。達明將撒出去的漁網控制在直徑約五公尺的範圍內，當網子下沉時，么哥就迅速溜過頂端的小開口潛進網中。

牠會從石頭下與縫隙中把魚趕出，讓牠們浮上水面，有時候一條魚可以重達十公斤。然後達明會用小塊新鮮魚肉獎賞么哥。順利的話達明可以在幾小時內抓到超過五十公斤的魚。

「你知道嗎，水獺對治療腎臟治療很有幫助。牠的排泄物，糞便，仍然很值錢。曬乾後每公斤可以賣五十元人民幣。我存了好幾袋等買家來收購，」達明驕傲地說。

of Yao Ge. Immediately Yao Ge folded both his fore limbs backward, hugging them by the sides of his body. Today, neither of Daming's twin sons is willing to learn the trade. They found the life of an otter fisherman simply too hard.

Daming's brother Dayong, 60 years old, rowed a second boat to facilitate our filming as we went out at night to fish. "Each of our otter is like part of the family. When mine died, I gave him a nice burial with a grave," he recounted. But as with everyone else, he has no way of replacing his loved one.

Daming told me that the otter is much treasured. Historically they were hunted for its superior fur. Chinese fishermen managed to domesticate them for fishing centuries ago. Even Marco Polo mentioned such a fishing method in his account of his travels. Using a cast net, Daming would throw it over an area about five meters in diameter. As the net sank, Yao Ge would quickly slide through a small opening on the top and dive into the net.

Wang Daming with Yao Ge / 王達明與么哥   Yao Ge ready for action / 么哥準備好大顯身手

我們在達明家旁邊的河塘裡忙了一夜後回來，這趟的收穫還真挺不錯。

我們在拍攝後的隔天早上離開，我的心中唱著最後水獺漁夫的輓歌。我一直有個疑問，或許永遠也找不到答案。當一個古老的習俗正在消失中，而這習俗又與大自然息息相關，與正在消失中的野生物種相關，那麼我們該怎麼在自然與文化保存之間找到平衡呢？動物權益與人權何者優先？

沒有水獺我們一定也可以捕魚，但是不能也留下一些水獺來馴化嗎？我想像自己站在雙方陣營中，都能為正反雙方想出一大串辯護。在今天這個充滿衝突的世界上，我們未必能找到完美的答案，但如果我們能站在一個舒適的立場去做判斷跟決定呢？這看起來似乎

A good size catch / 抓到大魚

Out of net with catch / 叼著魚鑽出來

Chasing fish from under stones and crannies, it would bring them from inside the net to the surface, at times with a single fish weighing up to ten kilos. In turn, Daming would reward Yao Ge with small pieces of freshly cut-up fish. A good night outing could net Daming over 50 kilos of fish, all within a few hours.

"You know, the otter is highly valued for kidney treatment. Its droppings, feces, is still worth a lot. It can be sold for Rmb50 for each kilo, dried. I have bags of it stored up for when the collector come by to purchase it," Daming recounted proudly. We returned in darkness after a good night's outing with some nice catch in a river pond next to Daming's house.

We left the following morning after the night of filming. In my mind, I sang the eulogy for the last otter fisherman. A question I always have may never be answered. When an ancient cultural practice is disappearing, yet it draws its lifeline from an aspect of nature, a diminishing wildlife species, how can we find a balance between nature and culture preservation? What comes first, animal rights or human rights?

Surely we can catch fish without the otter, but can't the otter survive also with a few being domesticated? I can imagine myself in either camp and come up with a long list of defences for each side, pros or cons. Those are questions we may not be always able to answer perfectly given our conflicting world of to-day. It seems nice if we can make judgments and decisions from a comfortable

不錯。然而，未必一直能夠如此。

在長江的這個偏遠角落，達明肯定希望么哥不是他最後的一隻水獺。然而，毫無疑問地，幾百年來世世代代延續的傳統現在正瀕臨消失……。

么哥不會是最後一隻河獺。但牠可能是王達明的最後一隻捕魚水獺。

position. Such, however, may not always be possible.

In this far-off corner of the Yangtze, Daming must certainly hope that Yao Ge would not be his last otter. A tradition that has lasted through generations and centuries is now at the verge of totally disappearing.

Yao Ge will not be the last river otter. But it may just be Wang Daming's last fishing otter.

Otter fishing c.1985 / 約 1985 年水獺捕魚

高原上的春雪

SPRING SNOW ON THE HIGH PLATEAU

Litang, Sichuan – May 14, 2017

高原上的春雪

帳篷在風中微微地顫動著。有東西敲打著防水外罩，聲音聽起來介於冰雹的硬和雨滴的軟之間，經驗告訴我這一定是雪。我懶得查看，因為我累得不想離開睡袋，即使連拉開睡袋的拉鍊都不需要。

我睡覺一向都不拉上睡袋拉鍊，方便我翻身以及避免幽閉恐懼。即使氣溫低於零度，我也經常裸睡，甚至喜歡把雙手放在睡袋外。我是牛年出生的，跟牛一樣固執，

Litang, Sichuan – May 14, 2017

SPRING SNOW ON THE HIGH PLATEAU

The tent fluttered a bit in the wind. Something was hitting the rainfly. But from its sound, between the hard noise of hail and the soft hush of rain, experience told me it had to be snow. I did not care to confirm it, as I was too tired to get out of my sleeping bag, unzipped though it was.

I have always slept with my bag's zipper down, so as to be able to roll and not feel confined or claustrophobic. In fact, I often sleep naked, even when the temperature is subzero. At times I enjoy having my arms outside of the sleeping bag. Born in the year of the ox and stubborn like one, my body is probably more like that of a yak, though without the fur.

The yak is known to have underdeveloped sweat glands, an adaptation to avoid the loss of heat under extreme plateau weather. I must be built the same way, as my body is hot, yet I hardly ever sweat, not even when I hike or exercise during my field work. As a child, I would only sweat when I was caught in some defiant antics. Otherwise, the only time I sweat was when I accidentally ate some chili.

Village near Litang / 理塘附近的村子

但我的體質可能比較像氂牛，只差沒有毛皮。

氂牛的汗腺不發達，這樣的演化是為了避免在高原的極端氣候下失溫。我的體質一定也是這樣，即使很熱，也不太會流汗，即便在野外工作時登山也不會。小時候，只有胡鬧耍寶時才會流汗。否則，只有不小心吃到辣椒才會時讓我出汗。

就在今天下午，我爬上附近一座山以瞭望野牛湖，並順便拍照。雖然在海拔 4300 米讓我氣喘吁吁，但是我還是沒有流汗。

太陽出來了，藍天中只有幾朵白雲。積雪的山峰離我們所在的山谷很遙遠。我們在理塘西方大約 70 公里，這裡是藏族古鎮與壯觀的長春科爾寺所在地。我通常只會停留在第七世達賴喇嘛的出生地，神聖古老的仁康，與我好友達賴家族的後代札西仁波切一起。

我們在融雪注入的高山湖旁邊紮營過夜。這是札西仁波切親自帶我們來到的隱密湖泊。有幾對赤麻鴨和斑頭雁似乎住在這裡，營地旁岩羊的頭骨證明了附近一定有這種生性害羞的羊群存在。湖裡有很多魚，在高原湖泊和河流裡常見的通常都是沒有鱗的魚。

Just this afternoon, I climbed up a nearby mountain to get a perspective view, and a photo, of Ye Niu Co, or Wild Yak Lake. While the 4300 meter plus elevation was taking a toll on my breathing, I did not sweat at all.

The sun is up and the blue sky has only patches of white clouds. The snow peaks are far and beyond our valley. We are about 70 kilometers west of Litang, a historic Tibetan town of western Sichuan and home to the Changchuen Ke-er monastery with its large ensemble of buildings. I usually spend time only at the sacred and ancient Renkang, birth house of the 7th Dalai Lama, with our good friend Tashi Rinpoche, a descendant of that Dalai's family.

We set camp for an overnight stay beside an alpine lake fed by melting snow. We were led to this hidden lake by Tashi Rinpoche himself. A few pairs of Ruddy Shelduck and Bar-headed Geese seem to have taken up residence here. A Blue Sheep skull lying by our camp gives evidence that the shy herd must be nearby. Fish are plentiful. Fish without scales are a common sight on lakes and rivers of the plateau.

But here there are also some big-headed fish with scales, easily a couple of kilograms each. I suspect they must be stocked by Buddhists who purchase them live in the market for release in the lake as an act of kindness. The action of introducing exotic and invasive species is actually against the law

但這裡也有一些帶鱗片的大頭魚，每條隨便就有兩公斤。我猜這一定是佛教徒從市場買活魚來湖裡放生，作功德的。引進外來物種的這種行為其實是違反自然法則的。許多這種魚死在湖邊，而原生魚種類卻開心地聚集跳水，完全無視我們的存在，即使我們靠得這麼近。

我們的司機兼廚師王健是個釣魚迷，他才下餌不到一分鐘，就有一條大約三十公分帶著黃色魚鰭的魚兒上鉤。拍了幾張照之後他趕緊將魚放回湖裡。這裡是禁止釣魚，尤其是當我們有活佛朋友隨行。釣魚或許可以偷偷摸摸，但是烹煮和吃魚可是瞞不了人的。

天色漸漸變亮時，我穿上冬衣鑽出睡袋。一爬出帳篷，發現昨天的綠地全都不見了。周圍世界全都被白雪覆蓋。在比較世俗的地方，雪像化妝品，可以遮蓋一切醜陋景觀。但在這裡，昨天的綠地像地毯，今天綠地換上了純白的新衣。

我的團隊有十四個人，雪地上點綴著黃色的帳篷。走出營地約一百公尺後，我在雪地上發現大大小小的腳印，於是我循著腳印來到湖邊，想必是動物趁半夜下山來喝水。大腳印很可能是屬於某種鹿，小的可能是其他夜行動物，貓、狐狸甚至小型麝香鹿。有經驗的野外生物學

of nature. Many such fish lay dead on the edge of the lake, while the indigenous fish were flocking and jumping with joy, oblivious to our presence and close vicinity.

Wang Jian, our driver cum chef, is a dedicated fishing enthusiast. He cast his line, and - within less than a minute - a fish with yellow fins measuring 30 centimeters took the bait. After a few pictures he quickly released it back into the lake. Fishing is prohibited, especially when our Rinpoche friend, the Living Buddha, is along with us on this trip. Fishing can be done stealthily, but cooking and eating cannot.

As the sky was getting bright again, I got out of my bag and bundle up. Climbing out of my tent, all the green pastures of yesterday are gone. Around me is a world of white clothed with fresh snow. In more mundane places, snow can act like a cosmetic and cover up all the unsightly scenes. But here, the green

Pulling camp / 拔營

Camping in snow / 在雪地紮營

家或許能分辨，至於我，只要有野生動物在我們身邊就
高興了。

最近馬匹很罕見，因為藏人早就改騎機車或開車了。由
於這裡幾乎沒有道路，所以占優勢的機車就處處可見
了。採收冬蟲夏草的季節剛剛開始，海拔 4000 高原點
綴著在地上匍匐尋找這種珍貴蟲狀真菌的藏人，現在這
種藥材每一條要價高達五十人民幣。豐收的時候一天可
以採獲十五到二十條，價值一千人民幣，春天來時有為
期兩個月的採收期。

要找到冒出地面的微小真菌子，這種工作對眼力是很大
的挑戰。通常小孩子因為身體比較小，更貼近地面，找
到真菌的成功率比成人高。當然，所有的收穫都進了父
母的口袋，然後好一部分捐給寺廟作為奉獻，讓寺廟更
加閃耀。

但這個早晨，我們的藏族鄰居不會在地上爬。下雪了，
冷到難以忍受，而且真菌又被蓬鬆雪白的地毯遮蓋了。
跟我一樣牛的，只有犛牛繼續固執地繼續活動。我看著
牠們挖開積雪吃底下的草，肯定也把冬蟲夏草搭配著春
天的草一起給吃掉了吧。

had been like a carpet yesterday, and today the earth has taken on a new coat, white and pure.

There are fourteen of us in my team, so the yellow tents dot the white terrain. I stroll for a hundred meters beyond our camp and I can see footprints, big and small. Following them I reach the edge of the lake. Animals must have come down the mountain in the depth of night for a drink of water. The large ones may well be a deer of some sort. The small ones could be of other nocturnal wildlife, cats or fox or even the miniature musk deer. An experienced field biologist could probably discern the footprints. As for me, I just cherish the thought that wildlife is in our midst.

Horses are a rare sight these days as Tibetans have long turned to motor-cycle and cars. But here where there are hardly any roads, motorcycles rule and are left around unattended. Cordyceps season has just started and the plateau above 4000 meters is dotted with Tibetans crawling on the ground looking for this valuable caterpillar fungus, an herb that is now command-ing up to Rmb50 per piece. A good day's harvest may yield 15 to 20 pieces, worth up to Rmb1000 for the day during the two month spring season.

Such work is a challenge to the eyes to locate the minute fungus fruiting body pushing up from the earth. Usually a child, with smaller body hugging

Tashi Rinpoche / 札西仁波切

the ground, has a better success rate than that of an adult. But of course, all harvests go into the pocket of the parents, and then a fair part continues on to the monasteries as offerings, providing more glitter to the buildings and statues.

On this morning, our Tibetan neighbors won't be crawling on the ground. The snow would be too cold to bear, and the white fluffy carpet has all but covered up the fungus. Like the ox in me, the yaks stubbornly persist. I watch them plowing through the snow, grazing from the pasture underneath and certainly licking up the Cordyceps along with the grass of spring.

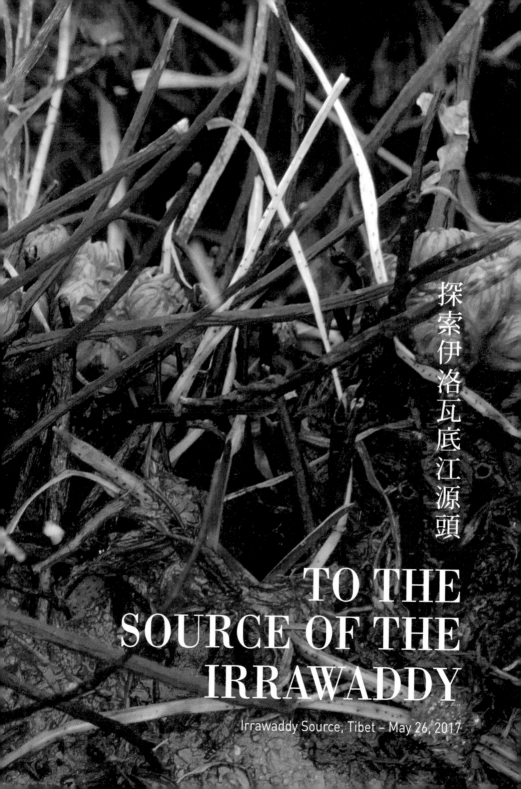

探索伊洛瓦底江源頭

TO THE
SOURCE OF THE
IRRAWADDY

Irrawaddy Source, Tibet – May 26, 2017

探索伊洛瓦底江源頭〈上集〉

座標：北緯 28°44'06"
東經 97°52'29"（28.7351N 97.8749E）
海拔：4710 公尺 時間：10 點 34 分
日期：2017 年 5 月 26 日

我回到紮營的基地剛過一小時，這裡位於海拔四千多公尺。營地異常地安靜，大家都累壞了，各自回到帳篷裡休息。我的大腿和小腿都很痠痛，漫長的下坡路上腳趾不停地碰撞靴子，讓我的腳趾也很痠痛。

但這一切都不重要了，因為我和隊員們登上令人暈眩的海拔 4700 米伊洛瓦底江的源頭，而且平安回來。在短短八小時內完成，並爬升了 700 米我的伽利略軟體提供的即時 GPS 與衛星地圖上的路徑，顯示我們走了 13.3 公里聽起來似乎不是太遠，但是在高海拔上爬這陡峭的山路，那真是最折騰人的 13.3 公里。

我從二零一四年就在籌畫這個壯舉，瞇著眼研究多張衛星地圖的每個小細節。道路、步道、村落、草原、牛舍、

TO THE SOURCE OF THE IRRAWADDY (PART I)

Coordinates : 28° 44'06"N 97°52'29"E (28.7351N 97.8749E)

Altitude: 4710m Time: 10:34 Date: 2017-5-26

It is now barely over an hour since I returned to base camp, at just over 4000 meters in elevation. Our camp is extraordinarily quiet. Everyone has retired to their tent to take a much-needed rest. My legs and thighs are sore. So are my toes, having hit my boots constantly on the long down-hill hike.

But all that doesn't matter anymore, as my team and I have reached the source of the Irrawaddy River, at a dizzying 4,700 meters, and returned safely. And all within a matter of eight hours, with a climb of 700 meters in elevation. My Galileo software which produced real time GPS and satellite map of our route showed that we have traveled 13.3 kilometers. That doesn't seem all that far, but taking into consideration the steep incline, it has been a most try-ing 13.3 kilometers.

It is a feat I have been contemplating since 2014, squinting to check on every little detail of multiple satellite maps. Roads, foot paths, village settlements, pastures, cow sheds, river systems, glaciers, peaks and mountain passes, I had

河流系統、冰河、山峰與山隘，還沒實際上路，我就對源頭這裡的地理與實體特徵非常熟悉了。我們花了兩星期在西藏高原上駕車，繞了一圈又一圈，爬上幾處高山雪地隘口，才終於抵達西藏東南部察隅縣的伊洛瓦底江支流。

在現今官僚繁文與政府限制下，西藏對外國旅客變得很敏感，我無法把中國境外長期配合的隊員帶進來，連台灣人都不行。所以，先前四次河流溯源同行的幾位好友與同僚，很可惜這一趟都無法加入。

所以我們團隊只有八個人，包括三位跟我們一起工作很久的藏族員工。袁新國（音譯）只比我小五歲，留下來看守營地。其餘人各自帶著乾糧和飲水，在早上七點十五分出發。我估計路程要走八到十小時，因為連接我們營地和源頭的兩條直線各自是 2.13 公里和 2.72 公里，加起來不到 5 公里。但是要爬升的這 700 公尺裡，我們必須走在陡峭的山路和許多之字形路段，所以自然會增添了不少距離。

出發前三十分鐘，有一群藏人經過我們營區要去挖冬蟲夏草，其中八個男人帶著簡單行李，加上一位看起來頂多十到十二歲的小女孩。他們要去的地方跟我們

Galileo reading / 伽俐略軟體的讀數

become familiar with all the geographic and physical features of the headwater region long before I set my feet on the ground. And now it has taken us
on a two-week huge circuitous journey driving around the Tibetan plateau,
scaling several high snow passes, before we finally reached the tributary of the
Irrawaddy River in Zayu County of southeastern Tibet.

Then there were also bureaucratic and government restrictions. Tibet has
become more sensitive for foreign travelers, and I could not bring my usual
team members from outside of China, not even Taiwanese. Thus, several close
friends and associates who have been along to four previous river sources could
not join me on this trip, unfortunately.

So there are only eight of us in my team, including three of our long-time Ti-

同一個方向，但會多過兩個隘口。他們會待兩個星期才回家，也有可能到一個月甚至更久。這些藏人是今年春天第一批從附近的曲瓦村出發的，因為隘口的積雪還沒有完全融化。

看到小女孩跟著大家一起出發，我真是佩服。聽說他們只花三小時就可以走到我們目的地那個源流湖。又估計我們可能得花四小時才能抵達隘口，那個隘口是伊洛瓦底江與薩爾溫江的分水嶺。我提醒隊員這個距離看起來似乎是不難走到，但是問題出在雪。如果積雪太深無法開路前進，我們就得撤退等秋天天氣乾燥時

Road in Zayu / 察隅的道路

betan staff. Yuan Xinguo is only five years younger than myself and stayed behind to watch our camp. The rest of us each took some dry snack food and water and started off at 7:15 in the morning. I had calculated the hike to last eight to ten hours, given that two straight lines with an angle connecting our camp to the source were 2.13km and 2.72km respectively, adding up to less than 5km. But the steep gradient and numerous switch backs needed to gain 700 meters in elevation added much more distance to our hike.

Thirty minutes before we started off, a group of nine Tibetans walked past our camp. There were eight men carrying simple packs and one young girl who looked to be at most ten or twelve years old. They were heading the same di-

Winding to pass / 蜿蜒的路況

再回來。在夏天雨季進來相當危險也很困難，因為經常有土石流。

上路大約半小時後，我們來到一片草地。這時因為高度的緣故我有點呼吸困難，但是步伐還算穩定，於是繼續前進著，但不久我就發現得開始爬山了。正在我開始懷疑自己能否爬上前面的長陡坡時，突然我聽到有鈴聲從背後傳來。回頭一看，有個騎馬男子快速趕上我們，他身後還有第二匹馬，被繩子綁在前面的馬上。

這顯然是天賜良機。我們一直想要租些馬騎去源頭，但也知道藏人早就改騎機車，他們的馬都在遙遠的山上放牧。況且，馬匹很少騎乘，可能相當野。但現在來了兩匹有鞍有韁繩的馬，真是天上掉下來的禮物。原來五十五歲的阿果帶著藏人的主食糌粑，要送到幾小時路程外的蟲草採集區。他也會留在那裡度過蟲草採收季。

我們花了點工夫說服、商量、議價，但終於談成，我們當中年紀最大的兩人可以騎馬。團體中最老的顯然是我，接著是小我八歲的貝瑞。我騎年輕的馬，三歲還有點野性，貝瑞則騎上溫和的十歲馬。這時機真巧，因為山就在我們面前，還好有馬救了我們，可以騎馬而非徒步上山。

rection as us but would go a couple of passes beyond to dig for cordyceps. They would stay for a couple of weeks before returning home, perhaps for a month or longer. These Tibetans were the first group this spring to head out from nearby Quwa village, as the deep snow at the pass had not yet fully melted.

Seeing the little girl marching along, I felt humbled. They said it would take them three hours to hike to the source lake that was our destination. They generously estimated that for us it might require four hours to reach the pass. That pass is the divide between the Irrawaddy and Salween watersheds. I cautioned our group that the distance seemed manageable, except for the snow. If the snow was too high for us to cut a path forward, we would have to retreat and come back in the autumn when the weather is dry. Heading in during the rainy season of the summer can also be quite dangerous and prohibitive, given the constant mudslides.

About half an hour into our hike, we reached a pasture. By then I was breathing a bit hard due to the altitude, but my pace was steady. Further ahead, I could see that soon we must start climbing. I began wondering whether I could make it up that long steep hill ahead. Suddenly I heard bells from behind us. Looking back, I saw a guy on a horse catching up to us fast. He had a second horse behind him, tied by a rope to the front horse.

This was obviously a godsend. We had been contemplating renting horses to

要不是有阿果，我們可能會走錯路，沿河而上進入一個險峻峽谷而無法再往上爬。有他當嚮導，我們於是順利往右邊沿著一長條之字形小徑前去。途中停下來休息時，我趁空檔問了阿果伊洛瓦底江源頭區主要支流的本地名稱。

他告訴我們左邊以冰河和融雪為起源的溪叫作 Moyu。中間這條稍長一些的，叫作 Chamai。最長的發源於高山小湖，也就是我們的目標，叫作 Dultong（又稱 Jiutong），北京的劉少創教授透過測量衛星影像也指出了同樣的地點。再往右，另一條較短的溪叫作 Depo。

Drolma & Agor leading / 帶頭的卓瑪和阿果

get to the source, but we knew that Tibetans had long since moved on to motorcycles and that their horses were on the loose far up in the hills. Furthermore, the horses are ridden little, thus can be quite wild. But here came two with saddles and harnesses, a gift from heaven. It turned out that 55- years-old Agor was carrying a supply of tsamba, the staple for Tibetans, to deliver to the cordyceps harvest grounds several hours away. He would also be staying there for the cordyceps season.

It took a bit of convincing, arm-twisting, and price-haggling, but finally we negotiated that the two oldest of us would get to ride the horses. Most senior in our group was obviously me, and eight years behind, Berry. I got the young horse, a bit wild at three years old, and Berry rode the mellowed ten-year old. This was perfect timing, as the hill was right in front of us, but we were saved, climbing on horseback rather than on foot.

Had it not been for Agor, we would probably have been on the wrong path, trying to follow the river upstream and into a precipitous gorge with no way to climb higher. With him as guide, we moved to the right and followed a long path of switch-backs. Along the way we stopped to rest, and I was able to ask Agor the local names of the main tributaries at this headwater of the Irrawaddy.

He told us that the stream on the left starting with a glacier and melting snow

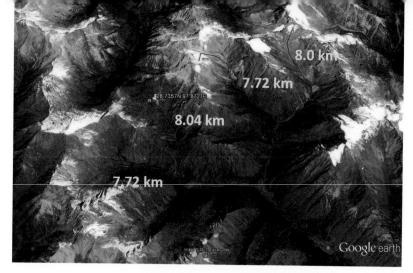

Source tributaries comparison/ 源頭各支流比較

夾著高山湖和隘口的兩座山分別是 *Hon Guangtu* 與
Rejacha。最重要的，伊洛瓦底江源頭的湖叫作金格拉湖
（*Jingla Co*，劉教授稱之為拉卡湖）。這些名字對別人
或許不重要，但對地理學家卻是很重要的資訊。

從一九八零年代初在 *NASA* 的噴射推進實驗室工作時
就認識的老朋友馬丁・魯澤克（*Martin Ruzek*），曾經
加入我去長江、湄公河和黃河的探源團隊。他負責我
們所有河流探源活動的遙測資料和科學分析。現在他
是全美大學太空研究協會（*USRA*）的主管，仍與 *NASA*
密切合作，為了支援我這次的探源行動，他測量、比
較過伊洛瓦底江的各條支流。他最終指引我們到源頭
那座高山湖的研究計算，對我們來說是非常重要且關
鍵的。

was called the Moyu. The one in the middle, slightly longer, was called the Chamai. The longest, leading from a small alpine lake and our destined goal, was called Dultong (or Jiutong), the same spot Professor Liu Shaochuang of Beijing pinpointed through measuring satellite images. Further to the right, another shorter stream was called the Depo. The two mountains sandwiching the alpine lake and the pass were Hon Guangtu and Rejacha respectively. Most important of all, the lake that was the source of the Irrawaddy was called Jingla Co (named differently from Prof Liu's Lake Laka). These names might be unimportant to others, but they are all relevant and crucial information for a geographer.

Martin Ruzek, my old friend since the early 1980s when he was working at NASA's Jet Propulsion Laboratory, had joined me to the Yangtze, Mekong and Yellow River sources. He has managed our remote sensing data and scientific analysis of all these river source expeditions. Today he is a Director with the Universities Space Research Association, still working closely with NASA, and has measured the various tributaries of the Irrawaddy for comparison in support of my endeavor. His ultimate calculation was instrumental and crucial in pointing us to the alpine lake source.

Martin however commented that a close and nearby contender, barely 40 meters difference in length, or two decimal points of a kilometer behind (8.00km versus 8.04km), is another headwater river. The two tributaries are just a

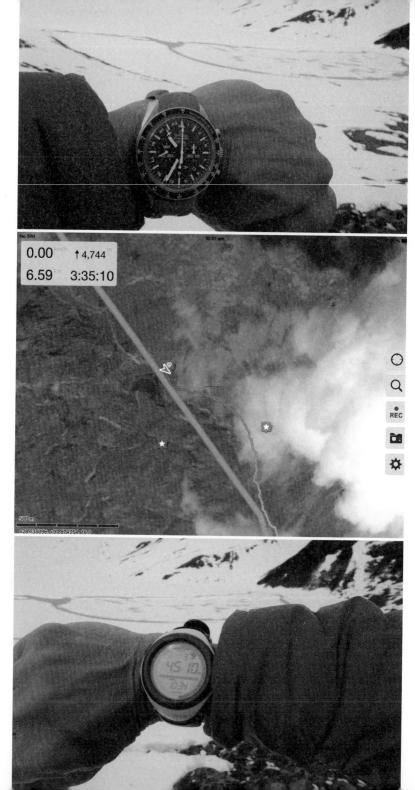

couple kilometers away as the crow flies. Such minute variations make it very difficult to determine a river source when both are in the same region, and with such small differences. Perhaps seasonal flow and size of flow are also debatable issues for consideration.

Previously when I checked online with Chinese sites about this region, I learned that a group of Chinese entomologists recently visited the area and found that Quwa village was a dead-end. Little did they know that this dead-end was also a life-spring, giving rise to one of the mightiest rivers of Asia. And had it not been for a marginal road which recently connecting Zayu in southeastern Tibet to Bingzhongluo of northwestern Yunnan, my expedition may require ten days or more on horseback.

But for now as we were riding this last stretch to the source, my remaining team fell further and further behind; understandable given the fast-rising slope we were now approaching. By now, three of our members were about half a kilometer behind us, and Wang Jian was a tiny dot still further back.

But our youngest Tibetan member, Tashi Drolma, was right behind the horses. She has lived all her life on the plateau. Her home is at 3200 meters in the village where the CERS Zhongdian Center is located. But even she found it a bit tough to be at such dizzying altitude. Here we were at 4500 meters

Arrival time / 抵達時間
GPS reading / GPS 讀數
Altimeter reading / 高度計的讀數

然而馬丁說附近還有個很接近源頭的河流，長度只差四十公尺，0.04 公里（8.00 公里對 8.04 公里）。兩條支流直線距離只有兩公里。這麼細微的差距又在同一個區域裡，差距這麼小令人很難判斷哪條是源流。或許季節性水流和流量也都是要考慮的因素。

先前我上中國網站調查這個區域，得知最近有一群中國昆蟲學家來過，發現曲瓦村是條死路。他們不知道這條死路卻是生命泉源，造就了亞洲最大河流之一。要不是最近有小路連接西藏東南的察隅和雲南西北的丙中洛，我們可能還要騎馬十天或更久。

但現在我們騎著馬走最後一段到即將抵達源頭的路，由於坡度快速的上升，其餘隊員落後我們越來越遠其中三個隊員落後大約半公里，王健則是更後面的一個小點。

但我們最年輕的藏族隊員，札西卓瑪，就跟在馬後面。她一輩子都住在高原上。她家在海拔 3200 米的村子，CERS 的中甸中心就在那裡。但連她都覺得在這種高度有點辛苦。我們在 4500 米持續爬升中，而她已經喘不過氣了。

and upwards, and she was out of breath.

Suddenly I heard a series of snorting sounds from the horse behind, which Berry was riding. It certainly didn't sound like the horse neighing or grumbling when tired. I asked Agor about it, and it turned out the bamboo basket behind the saddle was holding two small pigs. They were to be released as an act of mercy called "let live" once Agor reached his cordyceps harvesting ground. But at such prohibitive altitude, they would more likely become a sacrifice, soon frozen to death.

After 10am we finally reached the snowline. From here on, our move forward required breaking through the snow. For the horses, it might seem easy, especially because another group of Tibetans had gone before us just an hour before. At 10:30 and within 200 meters of reaching the top, it was snow all around us. Clearing a last ridge, I finally set my eyes for the first time on a frozen lake, a lake I had looked at intently uncountable times from space images. I looked at my Omega watch on my left wrist, the same watch I had worn to the Salween source. It was 10:34. I checked my altimeter watch on my right wrist; 4510 meters, calibrated as 200 meters lower, thus real elevation should be 4710 meters to be conservative, though my Galileo software showed our elevation to be 4744 meters. More importantly, I recorded my GPS reading as 28.7351N 97.8749E, a slight variance from what Professor Liu Shaochuang of the Beijing Remote Sensing Institute has established. Quickly, I

我忽然聽到後面貝瑞騎的馬傳來一陣叫聲。聽起來肯定
不像馬的嘶叫或疲倦時發出的聲音。我問阿果怎麼回
事，原來馬鞍後面的竹籃裝了兩隻小豬。阿果一抵達蟲
草採收場就要把牠們放走，這種稱作「放生」的善行。
但在這種嚇人的高度，牠們比較可能成為貢品，很快就
會被凍死。

上午十點過後我們終於抵達雪線。從這裡開始，我們必
須破雪前進。對馬匹而言或許很輕鬆，尤其因為另一群
藏人在一小時前剛剛經過。到十點三十分距離頂端不到
200 公尺，我們周圍到處都是雪。翻過最後山脊，我終
於看到了結冰的湖，這個我從太空影像研究、端詳過無
數次的湖。我看看左腕上的 Omega 手錶，它陪我到過
薩爾溫江源頭。這時是十點三十四分。我看看右腕上的

marked all these new data on my iPad Galileo map with a diamond icon.

From the ridge, I looked down twenty meters below at the source lake, a half-moon of frozen ice with its edges just starting to melt to reveal its crescent shape. Below my feet, the melting snow gathered as a wide stream about two to three meters wide. This tributary to the east of the lake is one of two larger streams in a bowl-shaped basin that drains into the lake, a rather stable body of water.

If however one were to be exact, these tributary streams, especially the longer one from the west but at this moment obliterated under heavy snow yet fully visible during dry season on satellite images as being 1.4 km further up the watershed, are the actual source of the lake. Jingla Co the lake, on its south side, drains into a larger stream, now called the Dultong, and quickly drops off the side like a waterfall into the gorge below. I would have liked to study the lake closely, as well as the streams that feed this body of water. But it would be dangerous to tread on snow or ice which may have empty crevices below. Such detail exploration have to wait, until the dry season come in autumn.

From here, the Dultong river changes several Tibetan names further down-stream (Zezhong, Azan, Gedao, Xhifui) before it merges to become the Ke-laoluo, and finally the Dulongjiang as it enters Yunnan from Tibet. And as the Dulongjiang leaves China into Myanmar, it became the May Kha river, above

高度計；4510 公尺，故意調低 200 公尺，所以實際高度保守地說應該是 4710 公尺，不過我的伽利略軟體顯示我們的高度是 4744 公尺。更重要的，我記錄 GPS 讀數 28.7351N / 97.8749E，跟北京遙測研究所劉少創教授紀錄的略有差距。我趕緊用鑽石標置在我的 iPad 伽利略地圖上記下這些新資料。

我從山脊上俯瞰下方二十公尺的源頭湖，結冰的半月形邊緣剛開始融化，露出新月形狀。在我腳下，融雪聚集成一條大約兩三公尺寬的小溪。這條湖東邊的支流就是在盆地裡匯入湖水的兩條大溪之一，水量相當穩定。

然而若要精確地說，這些支流，尤其是從西邊來的，比較長；雖然此時被積雪掩蓋，但在乾季的衛星影像上清晰可見。往分水嶺延伸 1.4 公里的那條，則是湖水的實際源頭。金格拉湖南邊注入一條較大的溪，現在稱作 Dultong，像瀑布般流入下方的峽谷。我很想要仔細研究這個湖，以及提供水源的這些溪流，但是此刻踩在底下的極有可能是空洞的冰雪，很危險。這探索只好等到秋天的乾季了。

Dultong 溪從這裡往下游換了幾個西藏名字（Zezhong，Azan，Gedao，Xhifui）然後變成 Kelaoluo 河，最後進入

Myitkyina it merges with the Mali Kha coming from the west and became the Irrawaddy, or locally the Ayeyarwaddy. It will continue its flow southward, passing through Mandalay to merge with the Chindwin when it makes its last stretch all the way to west of Yangon before entering its multi-channel estuary and into the ocean between the Bay of Bengal and the Andaman Sea.

Over the years, I have visited the river at various sections; in Tibet where the river is fed by multiple tributaries and with various names, later on as Dulongjiang I followed it into Myanmar, further on seeing it at the confluence of the May Kha and the Mali Kya, then from Myitkyina toward Bhamo, and from Bhamo to Mandalay and beyond. We have also sailed

Last stretch to source / 到源頭的最後一段路

雲南叫獨龍江。獨龍江離開中國進入緬甸後，變成了 *May Kha* 河，在密支那上方跟西邊來的 *Mali Kha* 河匯合變成伊洛瓦底江，當地人稱作 *Ayeyarwaddy*。它繼續往南流，經過曼德勒跟欽敦江匯合之後一路流過仰光西邊再進入多條河道的河口灣，在孟加拉灣與安達曼海之間入海。

這些年來，我探訪過這條河的各個段落；在西藏這條河有多條不同名稱的支流注入，在獨龍江我沿著它進入緬甸，再繼續看到它與 *May Kha* 河與 *Mali Kya* 河匯流，再從密支那前往八莫，從八莫到曼德勒與下游。我們也航行過伊洛瓦底江的主要支流欽敦江，溯河而上直到無法再航行。現在我們終於來到這個迷宮般水系的源頭了。

在我抵達源頭湖後不久，另外三個隊員也到了，開始到處拍照。又過了半小時，最後的隊員王健才到達山脊。這是他到過的第四個源頭，貝瑞也是，至於宋浩昆，這是他的第三個。而藏人卓瑪和周壽昌，還有昆明團隊來的李娜，這是他們的第一個河流源頭。我呢，伊洛瓦底江源頭是我希望造訪的河流源頭清單上第五個達成的目標。

the Irrawaddy's main tributary, the Chindwin, upriver all the way to where navigation is no longer possible. And now finally we are at the source of all this labyrinth of waterways.

Soon after I arrived at the source lake, the other three members arrived and began taking pictures all around us. It was another half hour before Wang Jian, the last member of our team made it to the ridge. This will be the fourth source he has reached, and likewise for Berry, whereas for Song Haokun, this is his third. For Tibetans Drolma and Zhou Shouchang, as well as for Li Na from our Kunming team, it is their first river source. As for me, the Irrawaddy source is the fifth checked off on the list of river sources I hoped to visit.

We gathered for a group picture with the source lake behind us. Each of us took turns to throw into the sky some Lungda, or Wind Horse. It is a religious offering scattered on the wind with blessings heading to heaven. For each of the four river sources I previously went to, the Yangtze, the Mekong, the Yellow River and the Salween, we brought along a bottle of champagne to toast the final moment of triumph. Every single time, I found the source water sweeter than anything else I drank. Finally I've learned not to challenge the natural taste and brought no man-made stuff to toast. As a ritual, I drank again from the river source. Once again, the water was freezing, and it warmed my heart!

Offering Lungda / 獻上龍打

集合後，我們依照慣例站在源頭湖前拍團體照。每個人輪流往空中丟龍打，意為風馬。這是一種往風中投擲讓祝福傳達到天上的宗教供品。先前去過的四個河流源頭，長江、湄公河、黃河和薩爾溫江，我們都帶了一瓶香檳慶祝。每一次，我都發現源頭水比我喝過的其他任何東西更為甜美。這次我學會不要挑戰自然的味道，不帶人造物品。一如往常，我又喝下了源頭水。還是一樣，水是冰的卻暖了心！

不像許多探險家選擇命名他們發現或初次踏上的地方，我只想到命名這個高山湖，科學上的伊洛瓦底江源頭，

Drinking from source tributary / 喝源頭支流的水

Unlike many explorers who choose to name places they discovered or first set foot upon, I only thought of naming this alpine lake, the scientific source of the Irrawaddy, by its shape as Half Moon Lake. Perhaps the local Tibetan name of Jingla Co is even more appropriate.

So far, everything ran according to script or even better. A guide and two horses appeared without planning. The weather was cool and conducive to our hike. We reached the source in just over three hours. As we began to turn back, however, snow started to drift down and fog was coming in.

For this expedition, I had gone back to work in the same way I had over thirty

根據它的形狀叫做半月湖。或許當地的西藏名字金格拉湖比較適當。

迄今，一切都照劇本進行甚至比劇本進行的更順利：一個嚮導與兩匹馬的意外出現。天氣涼爽適合步行，我們僅花了三個多小時就抵達了源頭。然而我們折返時，開始飄雪起霧。

為了這趟遠征，我跟三十幾年前一樣身兼多職。我不只是領隊，也是地理學家、作者、攝影師兼影片拍攝人。我們的影片與平面攝影師都剛好遇到家中長輩住院，還有一位就在出發當晚發生。所以我只好在體力允許下拍些影片。

離開源頭時我正在拍攝大夥兒拖著腳步穿過積雪的情景，結果突然聽到攝影機發出嗶嗶兩聲，接著就掛掉了。剛好跟我的體力一樣，沒電了！但是我知道我仍然必須專注在回基地的漫漫長路上。

雖然大多是下坡路，回程仍花了將近四小時。整個團隊大致集體行動，因為高度下降讓我們行走和呼吸輕鬆多了。回程中我們停下休息吃了點零食。在距離營地不到一公里時，我故意落隊放慢腳步，向外出發的旅程，我

years ago. I was not only expedition leader, but also the geographer, writer, photographer, and videographer. Both our filmmaker and cameraman were faced with unexpected personal emergencies when senior members of their families were hospitalized, in one case on the evening of our departure. So it was left for me to do the minimal filming that my limited energy allowed.

I was taking a clip of us pushing our feet one after another through the snow as we left the river source when I heard the film camera give out two beeps, and then it went dead. It just about coincided with the failure of my own body's battery, and I knew I must focus on making the long hike back to base.

The return journey took almost four hours, despite that it was mainly down-hill. The entire team stayed pretty much together as now the decline in altitude made life, and breathing, much easier. We stopped to rest and eat a bit of snack. When we were within one kilometer of our camp, I deliberately stayed back and paced myself slowly. For our outer journey, I needed my team and colleagues as companions. But now that we were within reach of safety, and I must take my own inner journey, reflecting on the special moment still lingering in my mind.

I thought of the old Chinese idiom that I learned as a child. It had stayed with me throughout my youth and adult life. "When drinking water, think about the source." This was repeated to me by my parents as well as by my teachers

要隊員們待在一起以策安全。但現在我們進入了安全範圍，是時候讓我看向自己的內心，獨自品味這個縈繞在心中的特殊時刻。

我想起小時候學過的中國古諺，從青少年起我就一直記得。「飲水思源」從小父母和老師總是向我反覆告誡。我的科學和地理老師教我怎麼用指南針，讓我能探索未知，我父母則是給了我道德指南。有時候我可能走偏一點點，但不會偏太遠。

我想起 2002 年時代雜誌頒給我的「亞洲英雄 25 人」榮譽，稱我是「中國最有成就的在世探險家」。那次表揚是我帶領兩次探索定義了長江的新源頭之後給的，但是兩次我都弄錯了。直到 2005 年我帶著團隊終於找到精確的，科學上正確的長江源頭。接著是在 2007、2008 和 2011 年，探索湄公河、黃河和薩爾溫江源頭。如今我們的功績又加上伊洛瓦底江源頭。這些成就只是長江的延續嗎？我不認為。探險是我終生的追求，這種成就是沒有頂點的。

找出河流源頭似乎是我這種探險家的完美工作。我缺乏那些征服山峰者的體力和勇氣。當我看著一座山，反而會猜想山的背後有什麼，想要翻過最低的隘口以滿

since I was little. While my science and geography teachers taught me how to use a compass, which allowed me to stray into the unknown, my parents had given me my moral compass. At times I may have deviated from it, but not far.

I thought of the Time Magazine 25 Asian Heroes honor bestowed on me in 2002, calling me "China's most accomplished living explorer." That accolade was given only after I have led two expeditions to define a new source for the Yangtze, and both times I had been wrong. It wasn't until 2005 that I led a team to finally find the definitive and scientifically correct source of the Yangtze. That was followed by the Mekong, Yellow River and Salween sources in 2007, 2008 and 2011, respectively. And now we have the Irrawaddy source to our credit. Are these accomplishments just a corollary to the Yangtze? I don't think so. Exploration is my life-long pursuit, and there is no pinnacle to such accomplishments.

Seeking out river sources seems a perfect undertaking for an explorer of my type. I lack the stamina and courage of those who conquer mountain summits. Instead, when I look at a mountain, I wonder what hides behind it and seek to scale the lowest pass in order to satiate my curiosity. So seeking out the sources of great rivers has become a life-long pursuit.

Some may ask, "What is so important about a river source?" I have met both Buzz Aldrin and Gene Cernan; the former was on the first Apollo Mis-

足我的好奇心。所以尋找大河源頭變成了終生的追求。

可能有人會問，「河流源頭有什麼重要的？」我當面見過艾德林（*Buzz Aldrin*）和賽南（*Gene Cernan*）兩人；前者參加了第一次阿波羅登月任務，後者則是登月的最後一人。我們都知道有月球，但太空人在探索任務開疆拓土的勇氣則延伸了我們的想像力。河流源頭也是一樣；對於沿河居住的成千上百萬人十分重要。

其他人可能從太空影像看源頭，但對地理探險者而言，地面實況調查代表一切。我從 1970 年代起就一直看衛星影像，當時我從在 NASA 與加州理工學院噴射推進實驗室工作的朋友們得到許多解讀上的協助。在 1970 年代是用 MSS 資料，然後我們進步到 TM 影像，後來是大片幅相機 *Large Format Camera (LFC)* 與幾代的太空梭

Ground flower at source / 源頭地上的花

sion to the Moon and the latter was the last man on the Moon. We all know there is a moon, but we admire the astronauts' courage in the pioneering undertaking of exploration that stretches our imagination. It is the same with river sources; it is relevant to hundreds of millions of people living along the river's course.

Others may have looked at river sources from space images, but for a geographic explorer, groundtruthing means everything. I have been looking at satellite images since the 1970s, when I got much help in interpreting them from friends working at NASA and the Jet Propulsion Lab at Caltech. In the 1970s it was MSS data, and then we graduated to TM images, and later Large Format Camera (LFC) and multiple generations of radar images from the Space Shuttle. Today, GPS and Google Earth are within anyone's reach on their mobile phone. Others may have worked on space images on paper, or in a lab and in comfort of an office, ground-truthing is essential for an explorer

Flower & Lungda at source / 源頭的花朵與風馬   Alpine flowers / 高山之花

拍的雷達影像。如今,任何人的手機都可以使用 *GPS* 和 *Google Earth*。別人可能靠紙上的太空影像,或在舒適的實驗室、辦公室裡研究,但是地面實況調查基本上仍靠探險家用傳統方式進行。並且,只有少數人有機會踏上這麼偏遠的地方。

伊洛瓦底江源頭之後,可能有人問「接下來要幹嘛?」那得保密。我們展開這趟伊洛瓦底江源頭探索之前完全不漏口風。出發前有幾個朋友和訪客在中甸中心看到我們。沒人知道我們要嘗試找出與定義一條重要河流的源頭。我見過很多在展開探索遠征之前,透過宣傳與記者會大張旗鼓的人。他們經常沒帶什麼收穫回來。一如往常,*CERS* 相信實績而非承諾。名聲與榮譽只是副產品,滿足我的好奇心才是主要目標。

不過在伊洛瓦底江還有件事要做。如同我們成功抵達幾條大河的源頭後,通常我也會到出海口去看看。那肯定會比找源頭輕鬆多了。在源頭,我喝它的水;在出海口,我會洗洗腳!

in the classic sense. Only a few will ever set foot on such a remote spot.

After the Irrawaddy source, some may ask "What's next?" That will remain a secret. We did not make any noise before embarking on this Irrawaddy source expedition. Several friends and guests saw us at our Zhongdian Center before our departure. None knew that we were attempting to find and define an important river source. In my time, I have seen many who made a lot of noise, through publicity and press conferences, before embarking on an expedition of exploration. They often return with little or nothing. As always, CERS believes in delivery, not promises. Fame and glory are but a by-product; satiating my own curiosity is the main goal.

One thing however remains to be done on the Irrawaddy River. As with other great rivers for which we managed to get to the source, I usually also go to the mouth, or estuary, to have a look. Surely that will be much easier than going to the source. At the source, I drank from its water. And at the mouth, I shall wash my feet!

上山下海飛上天

FROM MOUNTAIN TO OCEAN TO AIR

Dabang, Taiwan – June 26, 2017

上山下海飛上天 我的台灣探險

「妳有天可能會用得上，」我邊說邊把一盒解蛇咬的解藥遞給雪倫。「上次我來，不到五分鐘就看到兩條青竹絲。其中一條就在我們的房子邊。牠們非常的毒。」我邊說，邊翻過盒子讀印在背面的成分和劑量指示。

「嗯，妳看看——蜥蜴皮、蜈蚣、有毒植物等等。我猜被毒蛇咬到要以毒攻毒，」我指著成分。「還有劑量；剛開始二十顆，然後減到十顆，」我唸出盒子上的小字。

「但是等一下——孕婦請勿服用。蛤！為什麼不行？這樣說的話，這或許也能用來墮胎，」我挖苦說。「我不認為我會需要用到你建議的使用方式，」雪倫終於回嘴，還有點大吼。

但是對於我們來說，準備這些藥是必要的防範措施。我們第一次開放在台灣阿里山的項目接待學生，從香港來的八位學生和兩名老師。學生來自他們學校的動

FROM MOUNTAIN TO OCEAN TO AIR

A Taiwan Escapade

"You may someday find it useful," I said as I handed over a box of snake bite medicine to Sharon. "Last time I was here, I saw two bamboo vipers within five minutes. One of them was right at the edge of our house. Those are extremely poisonous." I added as I turned the box to look at the ingredients and the dosage printed on the back.

"Hmmm, look at that - lizard skin, centipede, poisonous plants and more. I guess it takes something toxic to remedy snake bite venom," I pointed to the ingredients. "And dosage; twenty pills for a start, down to ten later on," I read out from the small print on the box.

"But just a minute - do not use if pregnant. Huh! Why not? In that case, maybe it is also good for abortion," I quipped. "I don't think I would ever need it for your suggested application," Sharon finally snapped back, sort of barking.

But for us, the medicine's intended use is a necessary precaution. We are opening our Taiwan Alishan project site for the first time to host students,

CERS Alishan site / CERS 的阿里山據點

畫班。他們回去之後,會從這次學到的東西去創作動
畫。他們是來跟阿莫學習的,阿莫是阿里山深山的鄒
族原住民。

直到廿世紀初期鄒族還會獵人頭,現在他們只剩不到
四千人了。鄒族是獵人也是採集者,城市小孩可以從這
種仍住在山上仰賴大自然的山地部落學到很多東西。

第三天,學生們跟阿莫、畢尉林博士和雪倫出去郊遊並
且要過夜。沒有帳篷,他們必須學習搭建自己的住所。

eight students and two teachers from Hong Kong. The students are from an animation class in their school. When they go home, they will create animation films regarding a chosen aspect of what they have learned. They are here to learn a few things from Amo, a member of the Tsou indigenous tribe deep inside the mountains of Alishan.

Former head hunters until the early 20th century, today there are less than 4,000 of the Tsou people remaining. As the Tsou were hunter-gatherers, there is much for city kids to learn from such mountain tribes, who still live close to and depend much upon nature.

On the third day, the students embarked on an overnight outing with Amo, Dr Bleisch and Sharon. There were no tents and they would have to learn to build their own shelter. Food had to be prepared in the wild, after an extended hike in the forest. I, as the most senior in our group, would stay behind. With two days idling and few books to read, I knew I would get bored. My motto to students has always been, "If you find things boring, you are probably a boring person." So, I had to think up something to alleviate the situation.

As soon as the students left our site, I hitched a ride with Amo's wife down the mountain. An hour and a half later, I was at the highway junction. I had called ahead and met up with Ah Feng, a woman taxi driver I had relied on before. She would drive me for over a hundred kilometers to a coastal town in

在森林裡步行之後，他們還必須在野外煮飯。身為團體中最老的人，我於是負責留守。悠閒地度過兩天看幾本書，我知道我一定會覺得這樣很無聊。我給學生的座右銘是，「如果你覺得無聊的話，你很可能是個無聊的人。」所以，我得想個辦法改變狀況。

學生一離開，我就搭阿莫老婆的便車下山。一個半小時後，我來到高速公路交流道。我打了個電話給阿鳳，這位計程車女司機曾經載過我。而接下來她將載我跑一百多公里到南方的一個港口，然後我將搭上渡輪到台灣西岸的離島小琉球。果然，兩小時後，我順利搭上了渡輪。

到小琉球島的航程只要廿分鐘，但是這裡好像是另一個世界。我兩年多前來過這個六公里長的島，我很喜歡它的風景和安靜的氣氛。島上沒什麼汽車，但是有很多機車。騎車環島不用一小時。

這天星期五，我在碼頭租了兩天機車只花六百台幣（二十美元）。不久我住進一間只有八個房間的小旅館。這間星月旅館外面有鮮艷的壁畫，顯然是模仿巴塞隆納的高第。每晚台幣兩千五百似乎也很划算。

the south to catch a ferry to Xiao Liu Chiu, a small island off the west coast of Taiwan. Two hours later, I was at the ferry.

The ride to the island was barely twenty minutes. But it seemed a world apart. I had been here on this six-kilometer long island over two years ago and loved the scenery and the quiet setting. Hardly any cars were on the island but there were plenty of motorbikes. Going around the entire island on a bike would take less than an hour.

Dr Bleisch demonstrating camera trip / 畢尉林博士示範架設攝影陷阱

Snorkel herd / 浮潛的人群

然而我舊地重遊不只是想要騎車環島。上次來時，我看到綠蠵龜也聽到當地人吹噓曾經跟這些海洋巨獸一起游泳潛水。我也想這麼做。午餐後，我來到一家雜貨店買了泳裝和浮潛裝備。

It was a Friday and I rented a scooter at the pier for a meager 600NT (US20) for two days. Soon I checked into a small hotel with only eight rooms. The Star Moon Villa (Hsing Yue) with colorful fresco wall on the outside is an obvious imitation of a Gaudi in Barcelona. It seemed a bargain at 2500NT for a night.

However my desire for a revisit wasn't just to ride around the island. On my last trip, I saw Green Turtles and heard locals bragging about swimming and diving among these marine giants. I wanted to do the same. After lunch, I stopped at a variety shop and bought a swimming outfit and snorkeling gear.

Tsai Cheong-yi, the shop owner, goes diving all the time, and offered to show me the best spot for seeing sea turtles. I didn't care to join any of the snorkel-ing schools that go out as a group of ten. So I was delighted to accept his offer. We made an appointment to rendezvous the next morning to head for the beach.

The next morning, we rode our scooters to nearby Mei Ren Tung (Beauty Cave) beach. It was only ten minutes away from town center. Tsai told me there are more than two hundred sea turtles around the island, the largest density in the world for a tiny island the size of Xiao Liu Chiu. Here at this small beach, not of sand but of coral stones washed ashore, there are always a few sea turtles staying year-round.

老闆蔡昌義經常去潛水，提議帶我去觀賞海龜的最佳地點。我根本不想參加任何十人一組的出海浮潛團體，所以很樂意地接受他的好意。我們約好隔天早上會合再去海灘。

隔天早上，我們騎著速克達到附近的美人洞海灘。距離鎮中心僅十分鐘的路程。老蔡告訴我小琉球周圍有兩百多隻海龜，以小琉球這種規模的島來說密度算是世界第一。這個由沖上岸的珊瑚屑而非沙子形成的小海灘上，終年都會有幾隻海龜停留。

雖然才早上八點，已經有浮潛教練帶著兩團各十人的學生來了。在水中要避免撞到他們需要一點技巧。但我還是在岸邊的水裡待了兩小時。潮水湧來，有些海浪讓海水變得混濁。老蔡跟我說在天氣好的時候，水是清澈的。水底下的珊瑚好像很白，不過卻沒有看到什麼魚。

老蔡似乎知道海龜喜歡待在哪裡，所以我跟著他前往海灣的遠端。果然，淺水中有一隻大綠蠵龜，在水下不到兩呎。但是浮潛教練一定也知道這地點，不久我們周圍就多出了二十個人。

Though it was only eight in the morning, two groups of ten students each led by a snorkeling instructor had arrived. It took some maneuvering to avoid bumping into them in the water. But I managed to spend the next two hours bobbing in the water near shore. The tide was coming in, making the water a bit choppy and a bit murky. Tsai assured me that on a nicer day, the water is perfectly clear. The coral below also seemed bleached and not many fish could be seen.

Tsai seemed to know where the turtles like to hang out, so I followed him toward the far end of the bay. Indeed, there was one giant Green Turtle in shallow water, barely two feet under water. But the instructors for snorkeling must also have known the same spot, and soon we had twenty some people around us.

They quickly formed a roped circle around this turtle, which bobbed back and forth with the waves. The two instructors kept telling their students not to touch the turtle, yet the pounding surf would push the turtle to all these novice snorkelers with life vests. Some girls would scream out in excitement each time the turtle touched them. The many people with rope literally cordoned off the area and kept the turtle trapped.

I backed off and waited until they had had enough fun and left the scene. Then I closed in and had my special moment with this beauty of the sea. With

他們迅速在海龜周圍拉繩子形成一個圈，隨著波浪上下浮沉。兩位教練一直叫學生不要摸海龜，但是洶湧波浪會把海龜推向這些穿救生衣的菜鳥浮潛客。有些女孩每當被海龜碰觸到就會興奮地尖叫。這些拿繩子的人圍出了一個區域把海龜困住了。

直到他們玩夠了離開現場，我才往前靠近這美麗的海洋生物，並獨自與牠相處。我把 iPhone 裝在簡單防水盒裡，拍了些海龜的照片，有些是牠浮上換氣時從水面上拍的，其餘則在混濁的水下。我能想像這個大傢伙如果離水一定超過五十公斤，但在海裡，牠可以輕鬆地漂浮在水面下。我近距離觀察牠後，我非常驚訝，原來牠的前鰭那麼長。

跟海龜相處夠了之後，我趕回旅館，因為今天這是星期六，所有好的旅館都被預訂了，我得搬去魷姨開的簡易民宿。魷姨是老蔡的阿姨，她從十三歲就在市場裡賣魷魚，半夜還要搭船出海捕魷魚，有時候一捕就是兩小時。因為一輩子都在賣魷魚也活到了六十幾歲，所以每個人都叫她魷姨。

隔天早上，星期天，島上到處都是遊客。我也該回山上去了。我搭上早晨的渡輪，計程車司機阿鳳從嘉義開了

Turtle encircled / 被包圍的海龜   Rising for air / 浮上水面換氣

my iPhone inside a simple waterproof case, I made a series of pictures of this turtle, some above water when the turtle surfaced to take a breath, others below in murky water. I could imagine this big guy must weigh over fifty kilos once out of water, but inside the ocean, it floated with ease slightly below the surface. I was surprised to see close-up how long her front flippers were.

After satiating myself with the sea turtle, I hurried back to the hotel, as this was a Saturday and all the finer hotels had been pre-booked. I had to move to a simple family lodge, belonging to Squid Auntie (You Yee). She is the real auntie of Tsai. At the age of 13, she began selling squid in the market after going far out at sea to catch them, at times two hours out by boat at night. With a life-long occupation and now into her 60s, she's known to everyone as Squid Auntie.

一百多公里來接我。但我還不想回去跟學生們會合。我
得先去高雄附近辦一件要事。

岡山是台灣最重要的空軍基地和軍官學校。最近他們設
立了空軍博物館展出飛機，包括許多戰鬥機和古董飛
機。其中包括「美齡號」專機（以蔣介石的夫人宋美齡
命名）。那是 DC-3 型的 C-47 運輸機，被改裝成豪華總
統專機，這台從國民黨在中國大陸的最後幾年到蔣政權
撤退來台的前幾年服役。

我一直想要看看這架飛機，拍攝內部的裝飾藝術，特別
是駕駛艙。我們在香港的 1939 年展覽館裡，有個 DC-3
模擬駕駛艙。但我們缺少兩側窗戶的照片，這趟剛好有
機會可以填補那個空缺。阿鳳的儀表板上有台 GPS 導
航，她輸入了博物館地址——致遠路 55 號。

The following morning, a Sunday, the island became extremely crowded with weekend tourists. It was time for me to head back to the mountains. I took a morning ferry and Ah Feng, my taxi driver, came all the way from Jiayi, over a hundred kilometers away, to pick me up. But I did not want to go rejoin the students quite yet. First, I must make an important stop near Kaohsiung.

Gangshan is Taiwan's most important air force base and cadet school. Recently they established an air museum with airplane exhibits, including many fighters and even vintage airplanes. Among them was the Airplane "Mei Ling" (named after Chiang Kai-shek's wife, Soong Mei Ling). It was a C-47 version of the DC-3, converted into a deluxe presidential airplane and used during the last years of the Kuomintang on the Mainland and into the early years after Chiang retreated and moved his government to Taiwan.

For a long time, I had wanted to visit this airplane and photograph its Art Deco interior, especially the cockpit. At our 1939 Exhibit House in Hong Kong, we have a DC-3 mock cockpit. But we are missing pictures of the two side windows, and this visit offered an opportunity to fill that gap. Ah Feng had her GPS map on the dashboard all the time and she punched in the address of the museum – No. 55 Jie Yuan Road.

After we passed Kaohsiung and arrived at Gangshan, we drove toward the address. But as we got to the walled compound, the GPS tracking was lost.

HM in mock DC-3 cockpit / HM 在 DC-3 的模擬駕駛艙

我們經過高雄抵達岡山，隨即前往這個地址。但是當我們到了這個圍牆圍住的建築物後，GPS 導航頓時失靈了。然後我查看我的 iPad 伽利略軟體，衛星影像也是模糊的。我忽然想起來大多數軍事基地基於機密，這些資訊都會被擋掉。

但是我實在很走運。阿鳳說她的丈夫二十幾年前是這個空軍基地的學生，畢業後成為軍官，不過現在已經退休了。阿鳳趕緊打電話問她先生，他於是指引我們到空軍基地的後面，新蓋的博物館就在跑道旁。身為老人，我享受了門票半價的入場優惠。

巨大的展覽廳裡有很多架老飛機吊在空中，包括早期雙翼機和小型噴射機。我的目光立刻被地面上那架白色 C-47 吸引，兩側有藍條紋。「美齡」這個名字就印在駕駛艙窗子後面。我跟一個導覽員詢問可不可以進去參觀。

我很沮喪也很失望，如同其他所有展示的飛機，是不允許進入機內參觀。我只好在它底下走來走去拍攝它的外觀。還好有個安慰獎，C- 47 旁邊有台號稱飛虎的 P- 40 戰斧安然地停放著，宛如沉睡的老虎。

"Mei Ling" in foreground / 「美齡號」

I checked my iPad with the Galileo software and again the satellite blurred when I got to the area of the air base. Suddenly I realized that most military bases are blurred, out of courtesy and respect to host governments.

But serendipity kicked in. Ah Feng said her husband was a cadet at this air-base over twenty years ago, graduating as an officer, although now retired from the air force. Quickly she got him on the phone and he readily directed us to the back side of the air base where the new museum was situated next to the airstrip. As a senior, I got in for half price.

The huge exhibit hall had many older airplanes suspended mid-air, including early bi-planes and smaller jets. My eyes immediately caught sight of the white C-47 sitting on the ground, with blue stripes on its side. The name "Mei

還有另一個意外的安慰獎，或許比 C-47 與 P-40 更罕見的，是幾架屬於中華人民共和國空軍的飛機。其中有架 IL-28 獵兔犬式輕型轟炸機漆成綠色帶著顆紅星，星星裡面還印著八一字樣。那是中國軍隊的標誌。機尾突出兩支槍，飛行中砲手會擠在這裡。這架俄製的飛機於 1965 年由三名機組人員從中國投誠台灣。

另外三架中國軍機是一架米格 15 與兩架米格 19。米格 15 在 1962 年投誠，另兩架米格 19 則分別在 1987 與 1989 年。中英對照的說明描述了規格，彈藥火力，每個型號的性能，飛過台灣海峽的駕駛員姓名。然而完全沒提到每個投誠者皆獲得的一百萬美元的獎賞，這在冷戰高峰期可是會被大肆宣傳的事情，當年氣氛緊張，飛越台灣海峽可是一場豪賭。

我的思緒瞬間回到幾年前在新疆擔任主題演講人時認識的一位男士。這會議是關於保育及永續性，林毅夫也出席了。不像由西往東飛到台灣的米格飛行員，林先生是在金門島護衛前線的台灣陸軍軍官，隔著海灣距離福建省的廈門只有「很短」的距離。

「求救，求救（英文 May day），」遇難的飛機或船隻會用無線電發出這個訊號。當時也是 1979 年某個五月

Ling" was imprinted right behind the cockpit window. I asked one of the caretakers about getting inside.

To my dismay and disappointment, the airplane interior is restricted and out of bounds, like all other airplanes on display. I satisfied myself by only photographing the outside as I walked around its base. One consolation prize was next to the C-47; there a P-40 Tomahawk of Flying Tiger fame sat peacefully, very much a sleeping tiger.

Another unexpected consolation prize, perhaps more unusual than the C-47 and the P-40, were several airplanes on display belonging to the Chinese Air

P-40 Tomahawk / P-40 戰斧式戰鬥機

的深夜，林毅夫從金門游了兩公里向中國大陸投誠。後來他去了芝加哥大學接受諾貝爾獎得主的指導，取得了經濟學博士學位。最近我聽說，他當上了世界銀行的首席經濟學家。到現在，他的獎賞肯定遠遠超過一百萬美元了。

我也想到我離開小琉球的前夕，去探訪了一個面向中國大陸，緊靠海岸的舊碉堡。隱密的大砲與武器對準西邊的中國海岸。當時接近日落，我看得到遠方的夕陽和金色天空映出兩艘在台灣海峽巡邏的台灣軍艦。

現代的中國航空母艦「遼寧號」應該也帶著艦隊在海上，正前往香港參加慶祝英國殖民地回歸中國二十週年。它的戰鬥機隊應該不會升空，同樣地台灣的岡山空軍基地的戰鬥機也應該不會起飛。因為現在已經不像早年的政治動盪，不太可能在海上發生交戰。就像我面前的平靜海面——至少直到下一個風暴來襲。

Force of the Mainland, the People's Republic of China. Among them was an IL-28 Beagle Light Bomber painted in green with the Red Star and imprint of the numbers eight and one inside the star. That was the emblem of Chinese military forces. Two guns protruded from the back where the tail gunner would cram himself in in flight. This Soviet-built airplane defected from China to Taiwan in 1965 with three air-crew onboard.

The other three Chinese Air Force planes were a MIG-15 and two MIG-19s. The MIG-15 defected in 1962 and the two MIG-19s in 1987 and 1989 respectively. Descriptions in both Chinese and English depicted the specifications, ordnance capacity, and performance of each model, and names of the pilots who flew them across the Taiwan Strait. Nothing however was mentioned about the one million US dollars with which each defected pilot was rewarded, something much publicized during the height of the Cold War, when the air was hot and crossing the Taiwan Strait could be a deadly game.

My thoughts momentarily went back to a gentleman I had met some years ago when I delivered a keynote lecture in Xinjiang. Among those attending the conference on conservation and sustainability was Justin Lin. Unlike the MIG pilots who were flying west to east across to Taiwan, Lin was an officer in the Taiwanese Army guarding the frontline on the island of Kinmen, just a "short" distance across the bay from Xiamen of Fujian Province.

"May Day, May Day," as a distressed airplane or ship would call out on its radio. So it was on a May day and in the darkness of night of 1979 when Lin swam for two kilometers off Kinmen Island and defected to the Mainland. Later he was to gain his PhD in Economics from the University of Chicago under the tutelage of a Nobel laureate. The last I heard, he was the Chief Economist of the World Bank. Certainly by now, his reward must have been far more than one million USD.

I recalled also the evening before I left Xiao Liu Chiu. I was visiting an old coastal fort facing the Mainland. The underground cannon and ordnance position faced the coast of China to the west. It was near sunset and I could see in the distance the setting sun and the golden sky framing two Taiwanese warships patrolling the Strait between Taiwan and the Mainland.

The modern Chinese aircraft carrier "Liaoning" was also supposedly out at sea with its convoy, on its way to Hong Kong to help celebrate the 20th anniversary of the British colony's return to China. Its fleet of jet fighters were not expected to take to the air; likewise Taiwan's fighters from Gang Shan Air Base were not expected to scramble. An engagement at sea was highly unlikely, as now the political turmoil of earlier days had been eclipsed. Just like the calm sea in front of me - at least until the next storm arrives.

Line-up of MIGs / 各種米格機
Both Air Forces in same hall / 兩岸空軍共聚一堂

TARZAN OF THE MANGROVE FOREST

紅樹林裡的泰山

Palawan, Philippines – July 17, 2017

紅樹林裡的泰山

「叫我泰山就好，」洛伊一臉正經地說，他的額頭上有幾條皺紋。如果泰山是虛構的象徵，洛伊就是現實生活裡的化身，活生生地從叢林走出來。他的皮膚黝黑，兩側頭髮蓬蓬的，很像愛因斯坦老的時候那樣，但是烏黑，連鬍子也是。喬絲琳提議要幫他理髮。「不用，我喜歡長髮，甚至更長些。」洛伊說。

他通常很沉默，靜靜地做自己的工作。他的工作是什麼？漫遊在 *Maoyon* 河出海口的紅樹林，他家就在一條小溪的岸邊。從六歲起，這片紅樹林就是他遊樂、學習與生活的場所，這裡提供生存所需的食糧餵飽他和一家老小。現在，洛伊三十九歲了。

「洛伊，洛伊！」每當有緊急事故時喬絲琳就會這樣呼叫。緊急事故就是毒蛇。在我們外行人看來，所有蛇看起來都是有毒的。但對從小接受大自然洗禮的洛伊來說，牠們各個都不一樣。青竹絲和水蛇肯定牙齒裡有毒液。大部分的蛇只是看起來很毒，其實相當無害。不過

Palawan, Philippines – July 17, 2017

TARZAN OF THE MANGROVE FOREST

"Just call me Tarzan," said Roy with a straight face, with lines of wrinkles over his forehead. If Tarzan is fictional and symbolic, Roy is the real-life incarnation of that persona, right out of the jungle. His skin is dark, his hair wild, flaring sideways like that of Einstein in his old age, but jet black, including the mustache. Jocelyn offered him a haircut. "No, I like it long, even longer," said Roy.

He is usually very quiet, going about doing his job. His job? Roaming the mangrove forest at the estuary of the Maoyon River, where his home is on the bank of a small tributary stream. Since a child of six, these mangroves have been his playground, learning ground, and living ground, providing the subsistence food to keep him and his family fed. Today, Roy is 39.

"Roy, Roy!" Jocelyn would call out loud every time there was an emergency. Emergency that is, in the form of a poisonous snake. All snakes look poisonous to us novices, and the uninitiated. But for Roy, baptized by nature since childhood, they are all different. The bamboo vipers and water snakes certainly come with venom in their fangs. Most others only look

無論有沒有毒，被任何蛇咬到都可能會讓人歇斯底里。

就在兩天前，呼叫洛伊──洛伊的警報響起過。有條至少三米長的蛇被目擊蜷曲在我們的漂浮小屋底下。洛伊跑過來趴在地上查看房屋底下，他的長髮撩到水。那條蛇頭是三角形的，應該有毒，不太可能無害。兩三下，洛伊就用長竹竿在尾端做一個套索。他打量一下蛇的大小，調整了套索。我從河岸的制高點看，洛伊距離蛇的攻擊範圍只有一兩米。

洛伊故意去激怒蛇，希望牠會爬過套索。現場其他的工

Roy enters his playground / 洛伊走進他的遊樂場

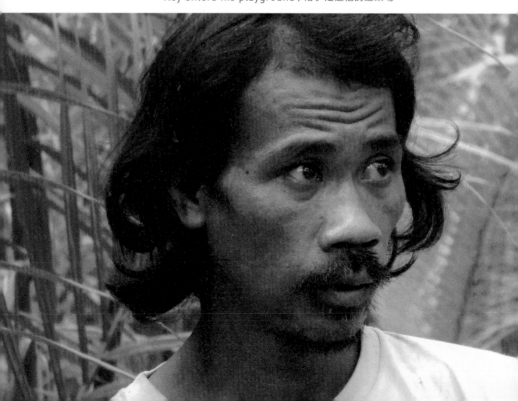

vicious, but are quite harmless. Yet any bite can bring one into instant hysteria, be it poisonous or not.

Just two days ago, the Roy-Roy siren sounded. A snake, at least three meters long, was seen coiled up below one of our floating cottages. Roy ran answering the emergency call and spread himself flat on the floor to look under the house, with his long hair brushing the water. The snake had a triangular head, probably poisonous, unlikely not. Within a short time, Roy rigged up a long bamboo pole with a flexible noose on one end. He sized up the snake and shortened the ring to match. From my vantage point on the riverbank, I could see that Roy was barely within one to two meters of the snake's strik-

Long-hair Roy / 長髮的洛伊

人在背後設法把牠趕向洛伊。但泰山毫不畏懼，瞄準蛇。蛇察覺到危險，鑽到水中迅速游向岸上。牠在水裡將身體伸展開時，我看牠肯定不只有三公尺，可能有四公尺，或許更長。

泰山隨即跳起來追趕，綁在他腰上的彎刀晃蕩著。他拔刀出鞘，以突擊隊射手般的精準，往離蛇頭十二吋的地方砍下去。被切斷的身體蠕動扭轉，蛇吐出舌頭靜靜躺在地上。我們情緒還非常興奮，泰山已經轉身離去，任務完成，彷彿這只是一件小事。

我在一年前認識洛伊，當時我們剛買下三公頃的椰子園、紅樹林與棕櫚林。後來我們又買了旁邊兩塊土地，一塊在河的對岸，現在總共有十公頃，超過一百萬平方呎。當時洛伊是我的嚮導，我跟他進入紅樹林與棕櫚林時，曾遇到一個巨大的野蜂巢。當時我在遠處觀察洛伊如何赤手空拳，也沒有任何防護網，只戴個簡單的頭巾輕易地用煙燻蜂巢，之後切下一塊。現在，我的早餐一定會有蜂蜜。

洛伊曾帶領我們的首席科學家畢尉林博士和攝影師李伯達，深入沼澤地。濃密的叢林崎嶇坎坷，連最擅長使用指南針的野外生物學家都快招架不住。那時洛伊，紅樹

ing distance.

Roy provoked the snake, hoping it would crawl through the hole. Other work-ers on site tried to irritate the snake from behind, pushing it toward Roy. But Tarzan knew no fear, putting the snake in his crosshairs. Sensing danger, the snake went for the water and quickly swam to shore. As it stretched itself across the water, I could see that it was definitely longer than three meters, maybe four, maybe more.

Tarzan jumped up on the chase, with his machete always tied to his waist swinging. Out of its sheath, with the accuracy of a commando marksman, he hit the snake twelve inches from the tip of its head. The rest of the severed body wiggled and twisted, the head lay still with its tongue protruding in its last draw of air. Before the rest of us quieted down from excitement, Tarzan turned his back and walked off, mission accomplished, as if another small job of the day was done.

I first met Roy a year ago, as soon as we purchased three hectares of coconut plantation and swamp of mangrove and nipa palms. Later we were to take up two adjacent pieces of land and one across the river, totaling now ten hectares, or more than one million square feet. Roy was my guide when I first followed him into the mangroves and palms to look at a huge wild bee hive. I observed from a respectable distance how Roy, with bare hands and a simple head scarf

林漫遊者，協助老畢找出架置攝影陷阱的最佳地點，紀錄哪些動物跟我們共享這塊土地。影像捕捉到的本土動物，包括一大群獼猴、麝貓、巨蜥甚至還有一隻石虎。

洛伊說除了被拍到的那些，這座森林裡還有很多其他動物。包括穿山甲，甚至連鱷魚和河獺都有。我傾向相信他。有隻泥蟹在沼澤上溜掉，洛伊立刻一腳踩在牠的背上，然後用手從背面將螃蟹抓起來。這隻半公斤重的蟹很快地就成為我的午餐。

他很謙虛地向我保證，用腐魚當餌，他就可以輕鬆地幫我抓到一隻巨蜥或鱷魚。即使沒有豹皮衣和註冊商標的叫聲宣告他的到來在，洛伊根本就是泰山。

Close-up snake / 蛇的特寫

but no net protective cover, smoked the hive before cutting off part of it to collect the honey. Now, that honey has become part of my staple breakfast additive.

In subsequent trips, Roy led Dr Bleisch, our Chief Scientist, and Xavier, our filmmaker, deeper into the marshes. The twists and turns among thickness of over and under growth can easily defy even a compass-savvy field biologist. There Roy, the mangrove wanderer, would assist Bill to identify the best locations to set up his camera traps, to record what animals are sharing their land with us. Pictures thus retrieved certified natives such as a large group of macaque monkeys, civet cats, monitor lizards and even a leopard cat.

Roy testified that much more life abounded in these forests, beyond those photographed. They include pangolin and maybe even crocodile and river otter. I tend to believe him. As a mud crab ran off from our path in the swamp, Roy quickly stepped his foot on its hind side, then caught it from behind with his hand. The half kilo crab would soon become my lunch.

He promised me, with matter of fact modesty, that with a stinky fish as lure, he could easily catch me a monitor lizard or a crocodile. Even without the leopard skin and the loud signature call to announce his arrival, Roy is every bit Tarzan.

Lunch delicacy / 午餐美食

CERS 迄今的巴拉望故事

THE CERS PALAWAN STORY

Palawan, Philippines – July 19, 2017

CERS 迄今的巴拉望故事

CERS 的 HM、畢尉林與貝瑞在 2014 年九月初次造訪巴拉望島。

直到 2017 年，不到三年的時間，CERS 多次派團隊去那裡進行計畫：探洞與開發、海洋生物的研究、對巴塔克人的文化進行保育與研究、調查小型山地部落的經濟發展、海岸與內陸漁民的普查，與協助貧困村民的小型社區計畫。

我們也拍攝記錄了這些計畫和其他值得關注的議題，同時設立一個設施完善的營運基地，也有艘可以出海的懸臂船來協助我們的工作。這個新的「巴拉望中心」將來也會成為探索、研究與教育的基地。

這一切都從 HM 在香港的菲律賓幫傭喬絲琳開始。她放假從巴拉望回來，給 HM 看了一支在她手機裡的短片，那是她小時候居住的島嶼的影片。這激發了 HM 的想像力，因為 CERS 正在擴展研究版圖到中國以外的

THE CERS PALAWAN STORY, so far

How Man, Bill Bleisch and Berry Sin made the first CERS visit to Palawan in September 2014.

Until 2017, in less than three years, CERS sent multiple teams to conduct several projects, including cave exploration and development, initiation of marine life study, research and preservation on culture and economic development of the small Batak hill tribe, survey on coastal and and island fishing people, and small community projects to assist disadvantaged villagers.

We have also documented these projects as well as other worthy subjects in films while setting up an operation base with full facilities and ocean-going outrigger boats to support our work. This new "Palawan Center" will also serve as a future exploration, research and education base.

It all began with Jocelyn, How Man's Filipino helper in Hong Kong. Returning from her home leave in Palawan, she showed How Man a short video on her phone taken of the coastal islands near where she grew up. It sparked How Man's imagination, as CERS was just expanding its reach to cover several

幾個鄰國和區域。

雖然南海，位於巴拉望西方的南沙群島爭議最近成為國際新聞頭條，但是 HM 覺得這些只是政治紛擾，就像爬山總有曲折迂迴。CERS 可以根據當地狀況調整參與的步調。我們聚焦是在這區域的地理、歷史與人民。機會來的時候 CERS 可以在這裡有些貢獻，就像我們其他的許多項目與基地所做的那樣。

Exploring cave in Palawan / 在巴拉望探洞

neighboring countries and regions of China.

Though the disputed Spratly Islands in the South China Sea west of Palawan was just flaring up into international front page news, HM felt such matters were just political switch-backs, not unlike uphill climbing with twists and turns. CERS can adjust our pace of involvement based on the situation on the ground. The geography, history and people of the region will be our focus. CERS can contribute as opportunities arise, just as we have done with many of our other projects and bases.

The initial survey up and down the long island of Palawan hightened our interest. Our further involvement and investment in time and money was well-founded on the diversity of both the natural and cultural heritage richness of Palawan. Meanwhile CERS filmmaker Xavier Lee, with support from cameraman Cao Zhongyu, is documenting every aspects of our work as it evolves.

Caving - Based on intensive and extensive exploration of two cave systems, the Hundred Caves and Dinosaur Cave, CERS cavers, led by Zhang Fan from Yunnan, helped map these caverns and gave trainings to villagers of the community about cave geology, as well as the biology within these caves. Our involvement resulted in a successful application to government by the village community in developing and opening of these caves to well-managed tourism, enhancing their income, previously exclusively from farming. CERS further

在狹長的巴拉望島進行的初步調查讓我們大感興趣。我們投入時間與金錢都專注在巴拉望豐富的自然與文化遺產上。同時 CERS 的影片製作人李伯達在攝影師曹中越的協助下，紀錄了學會工作的每個面向與進展。

探洞——在雲南大學張帆教授的帶領下，學會探洞人員嚴密與徹底地探索百大洞穴與恐龍洞這兩大系統的洞穴，不僅製作出這些洞穴的地圖還教育社區村民洞穴地質學，以及洞內的生態。我們投入的結果帶來的是讓社區村落向政府成功地申請開發與開放這些洞穴，進而妥善管理這些觀光產業。這個成果將會提高村民們的收入，在此之前他們只能靠務農為生。CERS 還提供探洞設備給工作人員，包括專業安全帽與頭燈。當然還有關於安全方面與永續經營洞穴觀光的教育訓練。至於一些其他的小投資則是用來強化他們的基礎建設。

巴塔克山地部落 ——巴塔克人的人口從 1960 年代的六百多人縮減到 2010 年不到三百人。以前他們是住在巴拉望中部的山麓叢林以狩獵、採集為生者。他們也會伐木與火耕，但是最近，巴塔克人轉為採集瀕臨絕種的貝殼杉樹，採集稱作馬尼拉硬脂的樹脂到市場販賣。

這個採集目標的轉變讓他們需要更深入森林中，這個工

helped in providing the staff with caving equipment, including professional helmets and headlights, and training in safety and proper sustainable cave tourism management. Other smaller investment supplemented their infrastructure building.

Batak Hill Tribe – The population of Batak people shrank from over 600 individuals in the 1960s to less than 300 in 2010. They were hunter/gatherers living among the jungle foothills of central Palawan. They also practice slash and burn farming. More recently, the Batak turned to tapping and collecting of marketable resin, known as Manila Copal, from the endangered Almaciga trees.

At a Batak village / 在巴塔克村落

作比先前生活方式更費力。他們的現金來源，亦即硬化樹脂，讓他們能買到衣物（受傳教士的教導）與白米，但是飲食卻不均衡，他們的熱量攝取減少健康因而惡化。

巴塔克人最大的村落坐落在 Maoyon 河上游，從世界遺產地底河流處延伸到蘇祿海，剛好從中間將巴拉望島一分為二。CERS 正在幫忙保存與紀錄巴塔克人文化，同時也體驗了讓巴塔克人掌舵的竹筏漂流，從他們的村子沿河漂流到 CERS 所在的入海口處的基地。

紅樹林與河口灣——在 Maoyon 河口附近有一小片原始河口紅樹林，不知何故沒被開闢成椰子園或養蝦場。河口的紅樹林棲地有獨特的多樣性，因為河水不同程度的鹽分，因此造就了讓更多樣物種生存的環境。這片森林大約七十五公頃，展現了完整的多樣性，從能夠耐海水的海岸紅樹林（Rhizophora sp.），到上游銀葉樹、木欖樹和水茄冬等大型樹木生長的鹽水森林。CERS 用攝影陷阱紀錄這裡的野生動物，已經發現了巴拉望的食蟹獼猴與巴拉望石虎，兩種是巴拉望獨有的特殊亞種。有三種翠鳥會在河岸捕魚，還有一對稀有的大灰啄木鳥在森林中築巢。此外，這裡也有完整的河口魚類與水生動物。

Such activities take them further and longer into the forest, a more strenuous occupation than their former lifestyle. Their cash crop, in the form of hardened resin, allows them to buy clothes (as taught by the missionaries) and rice, but sets off an imbalance in their diet, diminishing their calorie count and contributing to the deterioration of their health.

Their largest village is along the upper Maoyon River that stretches from the Underground River World World Heritage Site to the Sulu Sea, dividing Palawan in half along its middle. CERS is helping to preserve and document the Batak culture while experimenting with bamboo rafting trips operated by the Batak, floating from their village downriver to the estuary where CERS's operation base is located.

Mangroves and Estuaries – Near the mouth of the Maoyon River a small patch of old-growth estuarine mangrove forest remains, somehow spared from conversion to coconut plantation or shrimp farms. The mangrove habitats of estuaries are uniquely diverse, as they have variation of salt-levels in the water which support a greater variety of species. This forest patch, about 75 ha in size, exhibits the complete range of variation, from the saltwater tolerant coastal mangroves dominated by red mangrove (Rhizophora sp.), to brackish water forest upstream with large trees of Heritiera, Bruguiera and Barringtonia. CERS has used camera traps to document wildlife here, and has already found Palawan Crab-eating Macaques and Palawan Leopard Cat,

A sea turtle to be released back to sea / 一隻海龜準備被放回大海

CERS 已經擁有七公頃這片珍貴的森林，這座獨特的森林旁，我們蓋了科學教育基地，可容納十幾名教師與學生，以及一間實驗室，三艘獨木舟與其他研究教學所需的設備。我們的船可用於探索上游的森林、附近的海灘、海草床藻區與珊瑚礁。

海洋生物與珊瑚 —— 菲律賓的珊瑚礁面積超過二萬七千平方公里，其中密度最高，生物最多樣化的區域就在巴拉望，包括外圍的礁石與島嶼，例如世界遺產的圖巴塔哈群礁。

巴拉望位於珊瑚金三角的中央，是沿著赤道從南海延伸到巴布亞紐幾內亞，是公認擁有全球生物多樣性的熱

two endemic subspecies that are only known only from Palawan. Three species of kingfishers catch fish along the river banks here, and a pair of rare Great Slatey Woodpeckers nests in the forest. In addition, the full range of estuarine fish and aquatic animals exist here.

CERS owns 7 ha of this precious forest remnant already, and next to this unique forest, we have constructed a science and education base with space for a dozen students and teachers, a wet lab, three kayaks and other equipment needed for research and teaching. Our boats allow us to to explore the forests upstream, as well as the nearby beaches, seagrass beds and coral reefs.

Marine Life & Coral –Corals Reefs cover over 27,000 square kilometers of the Philippines, but the largest concentration with the highest species diversity are found in Palawan, including outlying reefs and islands, like the World Heritage Site at Tubbataha.

Palawan is in a central position within the Coral Triangle, a recognized hot spot of global biodiversity that extends along the equator from the South China Sea to Papua New Guinea, covering nearly 40 thousand square kilometres of seas, islands and coastal waters. According to some authorities, this region supports the highest diversity of corals and coral reef fishes on the planet. This rich marine life in turn supports over 130 million people, including the largest tuna fishery on earth, based on five species of tuna that spawn here.

區，涵蓋將近四萬平方公里的海域、島嶼和海岸。根據某些權威人士，這個區域供養了地球上最多樣化的珊瑚與珊瑚礁魚類。而相對的這些豐富的海洋生物也支撐了一億三千多萬與鮪魚相關的人的生活，包括地球上最大的捕鮪魚業，有五種鮪魚都在這裡產卵。

CERS 開始聚焦在巴拉望的 El Nido 或 Cawili 島。無論是在淺礁中浮潛，或沿著圖巴塔哈 100 米深的垂直珊瑚牆深潛，你都會忍不住驚嘆海洋生物豐富的色彩、造型與生活方式。CERS 在巴拉望與周邊島嶼跳島，短短兩週之內就記錄了至少 326 個魚種。其他的研究單位在這 332 平方公里世界遺產圖巴塔哈辨識出 379 種魚和 46 種珊瑚。

很清楚地，巴拉望的珊瑚礁不僅是觀光與漁業的重要基礎，這裡獨特無價的自然生態，也是世界上重要的資產。但是，如同我們在綠島目睹的，巴拉望的珊瑚礁正遭受來自炸魚、盜捕巨蛤、拖網與下錨、延繩釣和用自製魚叉槍過度捕撈的嚴重傷害。最糟糕的是，根據過去資料推測未來海面溫度，在極端溫度的壓力下造成珊瑚白化，可能導致未來幾十年區域內大多數或全部珊瑚礁死亡。我們都有責任去保護巴拉望無價的珊瑚礁生態系，CERS 將在保育的部分更加努力以做出貢獻。

Snorkelling among the shallow reefs of Palawan's El Nido or Cawili Island where CERS has started focusing, or scuba diving along 100 meter deep vertical walls of coral at Tubbataha, one cannot help be struck with awe by the plethora of colors, shapes and life-styles of the marine animals. CERS documented over 326 species of fish during just two weeks of island hopping around Palawan and neighbouring islands. Other researchers identified 379 species of fish and 46 genera of corals in the 332 square kilometres of the Tubbataha World Heritage Site alone.

Clearly, the reefs of Palawan are not only an important basis for tourism and fisheries, but also a unique and priceless example of an exceptional ecosystem with outstanding universal value. Yet, as we witnessed at Green Island, the reefs of Palawan are under serious threat from dynamite fishing, poaching of giant clams, damage by dragging of nets and anchors, and overfishing with long lines and home-made spear guns. Worst of all, predictions based on past and projected ocean surface temperatures indicate that coral bleaching, caused by the stress of extreme temperatures, could lead to the death of most or all of the reefs in the region over the next few decades. We all have a role to play in protecting the priceless ecosystems of Palawan's coral reefs, and CERS intend to contribute to that conservation process.

Island Inhabitants and Communities – On our first few trips, we explored near-coast islands of Palawan, around Honda Bay and the Sulu Sea. These

島嶼居民與社群——在前幾次的旅程，我們探索了巴拉望附近的小島，洪達灣與蘇祿海的周圍。這些地方離公主港與羅哈斯很近，搭乘我們新造的懸臂船比較容易到達，我們在試航的時候嘗試過航行到這裡。

許多小島上大大小小的自然原始海灘是屬於私人的，已經被開發成渡假村，禁止一般民眾進入。然而，一些比較有歷史的小島仍然保有原始的漁村。我們探訪了蛇島、貝殼島、約翰遜島、綠島等多處。CERS 在約翰遜島購買了適當的浮潛裝備，幫村民汰換自製的簡陋裝備。

從 2016 年底，我們開始出海探索，在巴拉望東方，航

Children of Cawili / Cawili 的小孩

are near Puerto Princesa and Roxas, easier to reach with our newly constructed outrigger boat during its shake-down cruises.

Many of the gem islands with pristine beaches, big and small, are privately
owned and have been developed into resorts, prohibited to public visitors.
However, some of the more historic islands with communities remain fishing
villages. We visited Snake Island, Shell Island, Johnson Island, Green Island
and many more. At Johnson Island CERS provided funding for purchase of
proper snorkeling equipment to replace the rudimentary home-made gear the
villagers used.

Beginning in late 2016, we started to explore far out at sea, over two hundred
kilometers east of Palawan, to islands surrounding Cagayancillo where Jocelyn's

Mother and child of Cawili / Cawili 島上的母親與小孩

行兩百多公里，到喬絲琳父親出身的 Cagayancillo 島周圍的小島。我們選了 Cawili 島，從 Cagayancillo 搭船三小時，在這裡開始我們的研究與工作。1.5 公里長的島上大約住了一百戶人家，主要靠捕魚和養殖海苔維生。神奇的是，雖然孤懸海外，島上竟有淡水湧泉。

我們團隊也收集了口述歷史，Cawili 島的故事與傳說。在後續旅程中，我們提供小型太陽能設備讓每個家庭都有基本的照明。這是一個小島社群，CERS 希望在這裡展開其他項目時也能同時帶來正面的影響。

清澈的海水讓 Cawili 和附近的 Malayang 沙洲島成為深潛與浮潛絕佳的場地點。然而，現在 Malayang 即使在退潮時也是在海平面下，被上升的海水輕易淹沒，殘留幾棟架在高蹺上的房屋。CERS 也希望能夠記錄這個瓦解中的社群，他們或許是地球暖化的第一批受難者。

在香港有二十幾萬名菲籍幫傭。其中，只有幾十個人來自巴拉望。到 2017 年中，喬絲琳已經回家十幾次了，回去協助管理我們的項目。「老闆，如果海關問我為什麼半年內回去六次，我該怎麼說？」喬絲琳問過 HM。「就說每當我犯錯，雇主就把我趕回家當作懲罰，」HM 大聲說。

father came from. We chose Cawili, three hours by boat from Cagayancillo, to focus our study and our work. The 1.5 kilometers-long island has about one hundred families living on it, subsisting mainly on fishing and seaweed growing. Miraculously, though far out at sea, the small island has a fresh water spring.

Our team also collected verbal histories, stories and legends of Cawili. On our subsequent trip, we provided small solar systems to make sure every family would have basic lighting. Being a small island community, CERS hopes to have a positive impact as we develop other projects surrounding this island.

The surrounding clear water makes both Cawili and the nearby sandbar island called Malayang, a perfect location for diving and snorkeling. Malayang, however, is now submerged even at low tide, obliterated by the rising ocean. It has only a handful of houses remaining, standing on stilts. CERS hopes also to document this collapsing community, perhaps one of the first casualties of global warming.

There are over 200,000 Filipino domestic helpers in Hong Kong. Among them, only a few dozens come from Palawan. As of mid-year 2017, Jocelyn has returned home over a dozen times to help manage our projects. "Sir, what should I say when immigration ask how come I went home six times in half a year," Jocelyn asked of How Man. "Just tell them every time I made a mistake, my employer sent me home as punishment," HM exclaimed.

馬背上的朝聖與獒犬外交

PILGRIMAGE ON
HORSEBACK

Ge Nyen, Litang – July 30, 2017

馬背上的朝聖

與獒犬外交

多吉尼瑪有兩顆心。一顆來自母親，另一顆來自牠的主人，名字也叫多吉，意思是雷霆。第一顆心是出生時得到的；第二顆心則是在是牠滿三歲時。一顆在體內，另一顆在體外。如今多吉尼瑪四歲了，而牠的主人，另一個多吉，則是 16 歲。

我初次遇見多吉時，以為牠有個心形的刺青，或許是烙印在皮膚上。原來那是用木炭製成的永久墨水。多吉是我的旅伴，精確地說是我的載具。我第一次去川西高原上理塘的格聶神山朝聖時，那整整三天，牠忠實地載著我進出荒野。

多吉有發亮的褐色皮毛，漂亮的木鞍下墊著藏式鮮艷圖案的墊毛毯。相形之下，我的穿著就顯得樸素平淡多了。中午豔陽下脫到只剩一層衣服，陰天時多穿幾層。牠騎起來平順又安穩，即使經過沼澤或崎嶇路面也一樣。

PILGRIMAGE ON HORSEBACK
and Mastiff diplomacy

Dorje Nima has two hearts. One from his mother, the other from his master, also named Dorje, meaning thunderbolt. The former heart, he received at birth. The latter, when he turned three years old. One is inside his body, the other outside. Today Dorje Nima is four years old, and his master, the other Dorje, 16.

When I first met Dorje, I thought he had a heart-shaped tattoo, perhaps burnt into his skin. It turned out it was permanent ink made from charcoal. Dorje is my traveling companion, or to be exact my carrier. For three entire days as I made my first pilgrimage to Ge Nyen, a sacred mountain in Litang County high on the plateau of western Sichuan, he faithfully carried me in and out of the wilderness.

Dorje has a shiny coat of brown skin, matched by a nice wooden saddle over a saddle blanket with colorful Tibetan motifs. By comparison, my outfit was rather bland, stripped to one layer under the mid-day sun, or covered in several layers when overcast. His ride was smooth and steady, even when going

我帶著團隊正從設在新冷古寺的基地營前進。總共有十個人,包括兩個分別來自倫敦帝國學院和哈佛的實習生。我們的馬隊有十八匹馬,其中八匹負責載物資與帳篷。我們也有六個馬隊幫手,全是來自附近喇嘛埡村的年輕藏人。「附近」的意思是騎馬需要花上半天的路程。「年輕」的意思是從十六到二十三歲,除了領隊德培是三十二歲。他們不騎馬,而是陪著馬隊沿途一邊路唱著

Dorje with two hearts / 有兩顆心的多吉

through marshes or rocky paths.

My team and I were on our way from our base camp at the new Lenggu Monastery. There were ten of us, including two student interns from Imperial College and Harvard. And our caravan had eighteen horses, including eight for carrying our load and tents. We also had six caravan helpers, all young Tibetans from nearby Lamaya Village. 'Nearby,' meaning a half-day horseback journey away. 'Young,' meaning from the age of 16 to 23, all except caravan head Depei who was 32. They would not be riding, but hiking alongside our caravan while singing back and forth Tibetan folk songs. For the most part of the next three days, our team would be on horseback, except when going through narrow hazardous stretches or steeply downhill, when we would dismount and lead our horses.

Ge Nyen has been on my list of sacred mountains to visit for over twenty years. I first visited Litang County in 1982 and had since made dozens of trips through the region, yet never made a serious effort to detour from the main Chengdu-Lhasa route and make a pilgrimage to the mountain. In fact, before a motor road was constructed into Tibet in the mid-1950s, the caravan route from Sichuan into Tibet went through Lamaya and skirted the foot of Ge Nyen Mountain before dropping off to Batang and the Yangtze.

Ge Nyen is actually the highest peak, at 6204 meters, on the outermost

藏族民謠，一邊步行。接下來三天裡大部分的時間，團隊都待在馬背上，除非經過狹窄險路或陡峭下坡，那時就要下來牽馬。

格聶神山峰列在我想探訪的聖神山名單上已經二十多年了。我在 1982 年初次來到理塘縣，之後來過這個區域幾十次，但是從未真正設法離開從成都到拉薩的幹道，繞路前往神山朝聖。事實上，進入西藏的公路在 1950 年代中期建好之前，要從四川進入西藏的路線都會經過喇嘛埡村繞過格聶峰山腳，再然後就是巴塘與長江。

6204 米的格聶神山是以同心圓形狀與另外十三座高山座落在一起，祂在同心圓的最外面，也是最高的。從我盯著好幾天的衛星影像觀看，祂終年的積雪看起來好像白色的人腦，只有一條窄小的山谷穿過祂的內部。

事實上，格聶神山算是四川省第三高峰，次於 7556 米的貢嘎山和 6250 米的四姑娘山，高過鄰近的稻城三神山，那裡是中國觀光客現在最喜歡的觀光勝地，從春天到秋天每天都有幾百輛車子的遊客前來。然而，即使格聶神山這麼高又與一位重要女神米堯朗桑瑪（Miyolangsangma）有關，但除了本地藏人外很少有遊

Lamaya village / 拉瑪雅村

ring of a group of thirteen high peaks curling together like concentric circles.
Viewed from space, which was exactly what I did for days on a satellite image,
it resembles a human brain of white, reflecting the perpetual snow over these
peaks. Only a small and narrow strip of valleys penetrates its inner sanctum.

In fact, Ge Nyen is the third highest peak in Sichuan province, behind
7556-meter Mount Konka and 6250-meter Siguniang, and higher than
the trinity of peaks in neighboring Daocheng, now a favorite destination of
Chinese tourists with daily arrivals of cars in the hundreds from spring to au-

Satellite image of Ge Nyen / 格聶神山的衛星影像

客前來。另外一座與此女神有關的山是珠穆朗瑪峰（埃佛勒斯峰）。

曾經有個例外是兩位美國探險家，知名登山家，在 2006 年 11 月來過。查理・福勒和克莉絲汀・波斯科夫在沒有官方許可與嚮導的情況下，偷偷摸摸地，挑戰這座神山。查理是位美國知名登山家，上過登山雜誌封面。克莉絲汀是航空科學家兼登山迷，她在知名的 *Mountain Madness* 創辦人兼嚮導史考特・費雪於 1996 年在聖母峰遇難之後，買下並經營他的公司，按照暢銷書《聖母峰之死》（*Into Thin Air*）的描述，還有七位登山家也跟費雪在同一天喪生。

tumn. However, despite Ge Nyen's height and association with an important female deity, Miyolangsangma, of which her only other mountain abode is Qomolangma (Everest), hardly any visitors come here except local Tibetans.

One exception was two American adventurers, reputable climbers, in November of 2006. Stealthily attempting the virgin peak without official permit nor guide, Charlie Fowler and Christine Boskoff made a secret challenge on the mountain. Charlie was a US climber of note and had been featured on the cover of Climbing Magazine. Christine was an aeronautic scientist turned climbing enthusiast who bought and ran the climbing company Mountain Madness, after the famed founder/guide Scott Fischer died on Everest in 1996, the same day seven other climbers perished, as the best-seller book "Into Thin Air" depicts.

The two experienced climbers, both Everest veterans, sent their last email to friends in the US on November 7, 2006, predicting their next contact in two weeks and their return to the US on December 4. They were never heard from again. Whether they considered their climb a challenge or a pilgrimage, as they literally were prostrating up the side of the mountain, is anyone's guess. But for Tibetans, to die on a sacred mountain during a pilgrimage is considered highly auspicious. As Charlie and Christine did not file for a permit, the Sichuan Mountaineering Association had to wait for a formal request from the US Consulate in Chengdu asking for assistance before dispatching a hu-

這兩位經驗豐富的登山家都是聖母峰的征服者，在2006年11月7日發出最後的 email 給在美國的朋友，預估他們下次再聯絡會在兩週後，然後會在12月4日回到美國。但是從此之後兩人音訊全無。他們視這次攀登為挑戰或朝聖就不得而知了，因為他們最後是拜倒在山壁上。但對藏人而言，朝聖時死在神山上是很吉利的事。因為查理和克莉絲汀都沒有申請許可，四川登山協會必須等到成都的美國領事館提出正式請求協助，才在12月中旬派出人道搜救隊。

徹底地搜遍該地區之後，搜救隊在拉瑪雅村發現兩名登山客留下的行李，意味著他們必定想要嘗試攀登格聶神山，這讓搜救隊伍聚焦搜尋行動。搜救隊歷經許多危險，12月27日在海拔5300米處找到查理的遺體並且確認身分。克莉絲汀的遺體一直到2007年7月才找到。顯然兩人都死於雪崩。

同一位神山之神米堯朗桑瑪或許在他們循著明確的路線攀登聖母峰時大發慈悲，但是決定在他們最後一次的攀爬送他們去投胎。這可以解讀為哀傷或圓滿的結局，他們轟動了全球登山界，卻不在乎中國的登山規定和當地藏人的精神傳統。希望這個事件能讓未來的登山客與探險家有所省思。

Caravan on the move / 移動中的馬隊

manitarian search team in the middle of December.

After an exhaustive search of the region, the rescue team discovered the two climbers' left luggage at Lamaya village, suggesting that they must have attempted Ge Nyen peak and allowing the team to focus their search. Charlie's body was discovered, despite much personal hazards to the search team, and identified on December 27 at an elevation of 5300 meters. Christine's body was not discovered until July 2007. It was obvious that both perished during an avalanche.

The same sacred mountain deity Miyolangsangma may have shown mercy during their Everest climb on a well-defined route, but decided to escort them

山頂上有給登山家的挑戰，同時山腳下也有其他爭議的事務。即使在精神領域，也有歷史和當前的敵對、矛盾和競爭。我們的基地營設在海拔 3900 米處，旁邊是新建、規模龐大的寺廟建築。這就是冷古寺。騎馬走一個小時還有另一座冷古寺，大殿和僧房都比較老舊與簡陋。

新寺廟是由巴塘來的仁波切（轉世喇嘛）主持，而舊寺由理塘來的仁波切管理。雖然兩者同屬格魯巴教派（黃教），但是目前正在互相競爭香客與信徒。爭論不時浮上檯面，需要政府介入仲裁。目前正在建造柏油路以便未來可以更容易進入神山，這種爭論只會更激烈而不會平息，因為成為宗教中心代表可能帶來豐厚的財富。

我在比較道地和原始的舊冷古寺停留。大殿鎖住了，喇嘛們也不在。不過入口的壁畫上有四位守護天王、曼荼羅及其他神明。我們看到一大群岩羊在寺廟外圍逗留。這些山羊通常很害羞會躲人。但在這裡，牠們像是被人養的一樣溫馴，我們可以走近到距離牠們幾公尺的地方也不會驚動牠們。許多西藏的聖地都是這樣，人與動物可以和平共享大自然。

to their next life on their last climb. It may be interpreted as a sad or happy ending, sensitive for the world's climbing community, insensitive to China's climbing regulations and the spiritual traditions of local Tibetans. Hopefully, this incident would lead to some reflections from future climbers and adventurers.

While challenges are up the mountain for climbers, there are other matters of contention in the foothills. Even on the spiritual realm, there are historical and contemporary rivalries, contradictions and contests. Our base camp was set at an elevation of 3900 meters, next to a newly built monastery complex with a large ensemble of buildings. It is called Lenggu monastery. Another hour further on horseback was another Lenggu monastery, older and more modest in its assembly hall and monks' quarters.

The new monastery is headed by a Rinpoche (Reincarnated Lama) from Batang, whereas the old monastery is ruled by a Rinpoche from Litang. Though both are of the same Gelugpa (Yellow) Sect, they are currently competing for supplicants and followers. The contest comes to the surface now and then and requires government arbitration. As a paved road is being built for future easier access into the sacred mountain, such contention will only rise rather than subside, as religious centers may soon become more lucrative financial centers.

Cloud over new Lenggu monastery / 新冷古寺上空的雲

I made a stop at the old Lenggu monastery, more authentic and original. The assembly hall was locked and the monks away. But the entrance had murals of the four guardian kings as well as mandalas and other deities. We saw a sizable flock of blue sheep lingering around the edge of the monastery. These mountain sheep are usually very shy and avoid humans. But here, they were tame like domestic sheep, and we could walk up to within a few meters without alarming them. Such is the case with many Tibetan sacred sites where man and animals both share the nature around them peacefully.

We set up our advanced camp at an elevation of 4151 meters. Our caravan helpers also set up their tents a short distance from us and kept a watchful eye over the horses grazing about the high pasture. The fog came and went, the sun shined and next minute rain fell. But over the three-day period, we had mostly an overcast sky. The high country above us however revealed that snow had fallen during the night with a fresh coat of white, from the perpetual snow on the peaks to gradual withering downward in grades of white.

我們在海拔 4151 米設立前進營地。馬隊幫手也在不遠處紮營同時盯著在高原上吃草的馬群。霧來了又去,一下出太陽一下下大雨。但是在這三天裡,多半是陰天。然而我們上方的高峰,新鋪上了一層白雪,顯示昨晚下過雪,從峰頂上的終年積雪往下形成漸層的灰白色。

在這個山區有很多山峰。形狀真是巧奪天工。景觀美得令人屏息,尤其當我們騎馬經過山谷抬頭仰望,左右雄偉山峰更是如此。這時是高原的夏天,草地上到處都有開花的植物。

也有犛牛和山羊到處漫遊。這些都不是牲畜,而是馴化過的動物被野放當作獻給神聖的山神。有些犛牛長得很巨大,脖子或角上常綁著彩帶,表示不可以殺害牠們。

隔天,我們騎了三小時來到一片高山草原上野餐。從這裡開始,我們得步行一個多鐘頭爬上一些岩石丘陵和曲折山路,爬升兩百公尺。到了 4468 米,我們抵達一座由上方冰河灌注形成的高山湖。周圍景觀還是很壯觀。我低聲禱告,往空中撒了一包龍打,也就是「風馬」。每張方形小紙片上都印了馬駄著神聖供品到天上去。

There were numerous pinnacle peaks throughout the mountain region. They were of such shapes as if sculpted by heaven. The landscape was simply breathtaking, especially so when we rode through the valley looking upward, while turning our heads left and right to take in the grandiose. This was summer on the plateau and flowering plants were everywhere in the high meadow.

There were also yaks and goats roaming around. These were not livestock, but domestic animals released to the wild as offerings to the sacred mountain deity. Some of these yaks grew to huge sizes, often with a colorful ribbon tied to their necks or horns, signifying that they should never be slaughtered.

The following day, we rode for three hours to a high meadow and had our picnic. From there, we had to hike on foot up some rocky mounds and switchbacks for over an hour and two hundred meters in elevation gain. At 4468 meters, we reached a high alpine lake, fed by glaciers from above. Again the panoramic view was spectacular. With a quiet prayer, I released to the air a pack of lungda, meaning "Wind Horse". On each of these tiny square papers was imprinted a horse carrying some sacred offerings to heaven.

Being the most senior in our party, two of the young Tibetans accompanied me, on my left and right, and assisted my descent back to where the horses were. We rode back to camp with the satisfaction that we had finally seen the front, side and back view of sacred Ge Nyen mountain. To circumnavigate it

Drolma with her two kids ／ 卓瑪和她的兩個孩子

身為隊上年紀最大的人，有兩個年輕藏人隨侍在側，協
助我下山走回馬匹所在地。我們騎回營地，很滿意終於
同時看到了格聶神山的正面、側面和背面。若要步行轉
山繞一整圈會花上當地人一個多星期，我們這些菜鳥可
能需要加倍的時間。我必須妥協，只轉一部分的神山，
希望神明能體諒我衰退的體力。

又花了一整天騎馬才走出了山區。從基地營，我選了
往西的一條無人小徑，讓我們可以從南邊與西邊看看

in a full circle on foot would have taken over a week for the locals, probably twice as long for us novices. I had to make do with a partial circling and hope the deity would be understanding of my diminishing physical energy.

Exiting the mountain took another full day on horseback. From base camp, I chose a little used route westward, giving us a view of Ge Nyen from the south and west. Driving up a high pass to 4600 meters, we entered the territory of neighboring Batang. The spectacle was again mindboggling, as we saw distant storms forming, then coming and going. We luckily bypassed any direct hit.

Just below the pass, we visited the camp of several nomads and were fortunate to meet Drolma, a most generous young lady who was willing to part with some of the items in her tent. These objects, mostly made from animal skin or woven from yak wool, will grace our nomadic exhibit back at our Zhongdian Center.

Below the mountain, we dropped to a valley and the village of Ge Mo. Here was more spectacular scenery, with karst hills of all shapes and on all sides. Though still very much among wilderness, our mobile phones started working again. A message and pictures came through that two Tibetan Mastiff puppies, one male and one female, had arrived ahead of us at our Zhongdian Center. These were gifts from the Qinghai government.

格聶神山。爬上 4600 米的高地隘口，我們進入了鄰接的巴塘縣。景觀同樣令人讚嘆，我們看到遠處有風暴形成，來了又走。很幸運沒有直接影響我們。

就在隘口底下，我們探訪了幾位牧民的營地，很幸運認識了卓瑪，這位慷慨的年輕女士同意把她帳篷裡的幾件物品半賣半送給我們。這些東西大多是用獸皮或氂牛毛編織做成，這些將會成為我們中甸中心的遊牧民族展覽品。

Mastiff Chili / 獒犬 Chili

After five grueling days in a car, these three-month old dogs made it to our Center. Perhaps due in part to the long travel, the baby male weighed only 21 kilos, and the female 15.

They are for restarting of our long-suspended project for breeding authentic stock of these giant canines of the plateau. Due to commercial speculation on these mastiffs over the last decade, as a commodity for vanity and wealth, it had not made sense for us to continue our project, which was first started in 2003.

Several months ago, word came through friends in Bhutan and their Agricultural Ministry that the current king of Bhutan would like to introduce some thoroughbred mastiffs into his kingdom. As China and Bhutan do not have diplomatic relations, perhaps offspring of these puppies would one day become ambassadors in bringing the two countries together.

But for now, I must hurry back to the CERS Center to make friends with these two puppies, before they grow in size and ferociousness beyond being approachable. Perhaps the sacred deity of Ge Nyen would see to it that our renewed program would become successful, bridging the two countries which are historical neighbors, but separated by the high Himalayas and modern politics.

之後我們進入一個山谷與格莫村，這裡有更多壯觀景色，四面八方都是各種形狀的石灰岩山丘。雖然還在荒野中，我們的手機又開始有訊號了。一封簡訊和照片傳來說一公一母的藏獒幼犬搶先我們抵達中甸中心。這是青海省政府送來的禮物。辛苦地坐了五天的車之後，三個月大的幼犬才能抵達到我們的中心。或許因為旅途勞頓，小公狗只有二十一公斤重，母犬則是十五公斤。

這是為了重啟我們暫停已久的計畫，復育這種純種高原巨犬。因為近十年來對這些獒犬的商業投機，把藏獒當作虛榮與炫富的商品，因此在 2003 年開始的項目覺得已經沒有理由繼續這個計畫了。

幾個月前，從不丹的朋友們與他們的農業部長口中聽說他們的現任國王希望我們幫忙引進一批純種獒犬。因為中國和不丹沒有邦交，或許這對小狗的後代有一天會成為拉近兩國距離的大使。

但是目前，我必須趕回中甸中心去，趁牠們長大變得兇猛難以親近之前跟牠們交朋友。或許格聶神山的神明會保佑我們新的計畫順利成功，搭建自古相鄰但被喜馬拉雅山脈與當代政治分隔的兩國橋樑。

Packed horse grazing / 馱運的馬在吃草

MEASURED DECADENCE OF AN EXPLORER

Kalewa, Myanmar – August 18 - 20, 2017

探險家的適當奢侈

探險家的適當奢侈

這一定是狗屎運。今天早上我打開電腦想要複習一下我即將再次見面的村民的名字，那個村子位於在緬甸與印度的邊界。那篇文章的日期是 2016 年 8 月 18 日。剛好一年前，我們再度來到欽敦江畔這個河鎮，準備踏上一年前的路線。說是巧合太過簡化。這次週年活動規劃的謹慎，其實是由一隻無形的手在後操作的，就像我當探險家的人生。

我們開了四小時的車抵達邊界。去年，因為當地發生瑣碎的種族事件，從緬甸德穆進入印度莫雷的邊界被關閉，市場完全淨空以免狀況升高為種族衝突。今年，市場人聲鼎沸。許多商品從緬甸進入印度，包括萊姆、檳榔、椰子，還有中國製造的消費商品轉運到印度。很多商店是邊界對面的印度人經營的。我們身為第三國籍者，是不被允許越過邊界，只有本地居民才能通過檢查哨。

然而這並未嚇阻我們這群充滿冒險與探索精神的團隊。

Kalewa, Myanmar – August 18 - 20, 2017

MEASURED DECADENCE OF AN EXPLORER

Serendipity it must be. This morning I turned on my computer to refresh myself on the names of some villagers I am about to revisit today, at the border of Myanmar with India. The date the article was written is August 18, 2016, exactly a year ago to date, and we are again at this river town along the Chindwin River, readying ourselves to retrace our steps from a year ago. Calling it a coincidence is too simple. This anniversary is prudently planned for, by some invisible hand, not unlike my life as an explorer.

It took us four hours by car to reach the border. Last year, due to a trivial local ethnic incident, the border at Tamu Myanmar into Moreh India was closed and the market totally vacated as a caution against the situation escalating into further ethnic strife. This year, the market is full of people and activities. Much of the merchandise is heading from Myanmar into India, in the form of lime, betel nut, coconut, and transshipment of consumer goods made in China heading to India. Many shops are owned by Indians from across the border. We, being third-country nationals, are prohibited from crossing the border, since only local residents are allowed beyond the check point.

我知道沿路有幾個點可以直接走路越界進入印度這邊的村子。我曾經這樣做過，也不會猶豫再來一次。中午陽光炙熱，我們廂型車的空調壞了。身為熟練但衰老中的探險家，我趕緊下令司機趁著午餐空檔去修車廠把空調修好，餐後一小時內我們繼續上路。

兩年前電信服務還是稀有的奢侈品，如今在大多數緬甸城鎮甚至一些小村已經很普遍了。我看到一個年輕人穿著反抗科技時代的有趣 T 恤。上面印著，「我不需要 Google，我老婆什麼都知道」。

Kuki Children / 欽族小孩

This however did not deter our group, filled with adventure and exploration spirit. I knew of several points along the road where we can simply hike across the border into villages on the Indian side. I have done it before and have no hesitation in doing so again. The mid-day sun is hot and our van's air-con has broken. As a seasoned but ageing explorer, I quickly order the driver to have the air-con fixed at a local shop while we have lunch, and within an hour after lunch we are back on our way.

While two years ago mobile service was a rare luxury, today it is prevalent in most of Myanmar's cities and towns, including even some small villages.

Rosemary's mother / 蘿絲瑪莉的母親

路口有間茅草小屋商店，我們停下來之後轉往印度側的 *Chang Pol* 村。約翰和安西婭，還有畢尉林博士和我們的緬甸生物學家蘇，選擇步行。約翰比我年長十歲，畢尉林小我五歲。但我們訂了三台機車必須要有人騎，所以我乾脆也騎一台。我們年輕的客人德瑞克和緬甸經理珊卓也上車。退休的匯豐銀行大班之前也是 *CERS* 董事的約翰邁步前進，我則是擔任探險的大班搭乘著機動交通工具，這感覺挺不錯的。兩天前我們探訪早市時也是這樣；約翰寧可走路，而我則是坐三輪機車。

蘿絲瑪莉已經在等我們了。有風聲說我們會再來她的村子。我的機車聲一接近老舊校舍，她就走過來迎接我。過了不久，團隊其餘的人也到了，因為從邊界公路過來只有一公里多。我們花不到十五分鐘時間，就從緬甸進入了印度的曼尼普爾邦。

「妳還是單身嗎？」我開玩笑問，想起去年蘿絲瑪莉怨嘆村裡沒有好男人，所以她一直單身。「我三個月前結婚了，」蘿絲瑪莉害羞地微笑回答。「我終於認識了可以信任的人，」蘿絲瑪莉又說。「他是我們同胞，欽族人，出身附近的村子，」她說。「他認識我之後，一直跑來找我求婚，」她更顯害羞地透露。

I am amused seeing a young man sporting a T-shirt short-circuiting the technology age. It reads, "I don't need Google, my wife knows everything".

At a trailhead with a thatched shed for a shop, we stop and head for Chang Pol Village on the Indian side. John and Anthea, as well as Dr Bill and Su, our Myanmar biologist, choose to go on foot. John is ten years my senior and Bill five years my junior. But we have reserved three motorcycles and someone must ride, so I may as well be one of them. Derrick our young guest and Sandra our Myanmar manager also oblige. It feels good that John, retired Taipan of HSBC and formerly a CERS Director, is marching on foot while I act as the Taipan of Exploration, riding on a motorized vehicle. The same happened two days ago when we visited a morning market; John preferred to walk while I took a motor trishaw.

Rosemary has been waiting for us. Word has gone ahead that we would be visiting her village again. As soon as my motorcycle roars up to the old school house, she walks up to greet me. Soon after, the rest of our party arrive, as the hike is only slightly over one kilometer from the border road. We are, within less than fifteen minutes, effectively inside Manipur State of India from Myanmar.

"Are you still single?" I asked jokingly as I remember that last year Rosemary lamented that there was no good man around, thus she remained single. "I

「你們認識多久後你才答應嫁給他了？」我問，心裡預期會有個保守的答案。這時我們走到了村中年久失修的教堂，她就在這裡舉行婚禮。「只有一星期，」蘿絲瑪莉回答。她立刻發現這個答案很不尋常而尷尬起來，揮手捶打我的肩膀一邊低頭笑。我決定不再追問細節。

我們的注意力轉向蘿絲瑪莉的父親法蘭西斯，他希望我們幫忙汰換的老教堂。喝著萊姆汁，這是他們庭園裡唯一的奢侈品，法蘭西斯招呼我坐下給我一條漂亮的繡花毯子披在肩上，同時用嚴肅地語氣提出他的要求，他的要求由他的女兒翻譯成英語。

因為這要求不過分，又是用當地的勞工建造，所以我們馬上就答應了。我們也交給蘿絲瑪莉去年她要求的書和文具，因為他們學校急切的需這些基本教材。之後，蘿絲瑪莉和她父親帶我散步到不到十五分鐘遠的鄰村。新教堂完成後這個小村子也會使用。欽族人都是基督徒，不像印度政府裡的官員是印度教徒。

現在 Chang Pol 只有十五戶人家。蘿絲瑪莉說很多年前她還小的時候大約有一百五十戶。政府想要把他們遷到內陸遠離邊界，所以士兵會來騷擾村民。大家都很害怕所以搬走了。七年之後，開始有幾戶搬回來，堅持留下

got married just three months ago," answered Rosemary with a shy smile. "I finally met someone I can trust," Rosemary added. "He's from our same tribe, the Kuki people, but from a nearby village," she said. "After he met me, he kept coming over and asked for my hand," she revealed with a bit more shyness.

"So how long have you known him before agreeing to be betrothed to him?" I asked, expecting a conservative answer. By then we had strolled to the old, dilapidated church in the village where her wedding took place. "Only a week," came Rosemary's answer. Right away she knew that that answer seemed odd and felt embarrassed, swinging her arm to hit my shoulder while laughing with her head down. I pursue the details no more.

Our attention turned to the old church which Rosemary's father Francis hopes we will help to replace with a new one. Over a cup of lime juice, served as the only luxury they have from their garden, Francis sat me down to offer me a nicely embroidered blanket, wrapping it around my shoulders as he made his request in a solemn voice, translated into English by his daughter.

Given the modest amount on request, to be built with local labor, we quickly obliged. We also handed over the books and stationary Rosemary had asked for last year, for their school is in dire need of such basic materials. Thereafter, Rosemary and her father took me for a walk to the next village, barely fifteen

Old riverboat in Chindwin / 欽敦江上的舊河船

的現在只有他們十五戶。附近還有另外三個欽族村落。
他們的語言很獨特，跟米佐族語有部分相似。不過，蘿
絲瑪莉英語說得很好，她父親也會說緬語。

天黑後許久，十點過後，我們團隊才回到 *HM Explorer*，
探險船停泊在葛禮瓦的欽敦江邊。在炎夏遠足一整天
之後，有空調的艙房真是舒服。我心裡一向認為如果
雅克・庫斯托還活著，也會認同現代探險家有這種奢
侈。我懷疑他的船，卡利普索號可能也有類似的設施。

minutes away. This smaller village will also be using the new church when it is done. All Kuki people are Christians, unlike their overlords in the Indian government, who are Hindus.

Today Chang Pol has only fifteen families. Rosemary said many years ago when she was young there were 150 or so families. The government wanted to move them away inland further from the border, thus the soldiers came to harass the villagers. Everyone got really frightened and moved away. After seven years, a few families began moving back, and today they only amount to fifteen families who persevere in staying. There are three other Kuki villages nearby in the vicinity. Their language is unique, and only in part resembles that of another tribe, the Mizou people. Rosemary, however, also speaks perfect English, and her father speaks Burmese.

It was long after dark, after 10pm, when our team arrived back at the HM Explorer, the CERS exploration vessel, docked along the Chindwin River at Kalewa. The air-conditioned cabins are certainly comfortable respite from a long day's excursion in the summer heat. I've always thought in my mind that if Jacques Cousteau was alive today, he would approve of such luxury for a modern explorer. I suspect his boat, the Calypso, may have had such amenities as well.

Such comfort on expedition is what I call "measured decadence," as explorers

探險中的這種舒適就是我所謂的「適當的奢侈」，因為探險家尋求的是知識，不是勞苦。許多貴族探險家與富裕的學者不只會同意，而且還很擅長在長途探險中準備這些設備。我們陸上探險用的 Land Rover 車隊確實提供了這些很基本的舒適，從用餐帳篷到折疊式廁所，甚至還有一次用到太陽能浴缸。

但是當情況不允許享有這些奢侈，每當有目的或天命在手上時，老練的探險家一定能夠忍受沒有這些舒適的設備。就在最近三個月，我騎了兩次馬，其中一次持續將近漫長的三天。在巴拉望我們新的項目點還在建造的過程中，我兩年來多次睡在陽台上不到兩呎寬的竹凳上，每次為期一週或更久。

在緬甸的 HM Explorer 上我們有七間全空調艙房，獨立廁所與浴室，衛星電話，電腦與印表機，大螢幕電視，聲納，氣象站，多種酒類的吧台，精選圖書室和展示間，充氣快艇，獨木舟，機車和八台腳踏車。另一方面，我們在巴拉望的懸臂船 HM Explorer II 只有一個開放式「艙房」。有時候，我們五六個人擠在船上的雙層床位，有些人寧可睡在銀河天幕下的上層甲板，或者在下雨和風暴時，睡在只有一點點庇護的油布棚下。開這 HM Explorer I 跟 HM Explorer II 這兩艘船航行我覺得都一

seek knowledge, not hardship. Many aristocrat explorers and well-heeled scholar types would not only concur, but excel in preparing for such measures on long expeditions. Our fleet of Land Rovers on land expeditions certainly provided such very basic comforts, from a dining tent to folding toilet, and once even a solar bathtub.

But when conditions did not avail themselves to such luxury, the seasoned explorer can certainly bear the absence of comfort, whenever a purpose or destiny is at hand. Just within the last three months, I have been on horseback twice, once almost continuously for three long days. At our new project site under construction in Palawan, I have over the last two years slept on a bamboo bench barely two-feet wide on a balcony many times, each time for a week or longer.

On the HM Explorer in Myanmar we have seven fully air-conditioned cabins, separate toilets and showers, satellite phone, computer with printer, large screen TV, sonar, weather station, bar with liquor choices, a select library and exhibit displays, inflatable speedboats, kayak, motorcycles and eight bicycles. On the other hand, our outrigger boat HM Explorer 2 in Palawan has only one open "cabin". At times, there are five or six of us cramped into it on bunks, while some of us would rather sleep on the top deck under a canopy of the galaxy, or, during rain and storm, under a tarp canopy with minimal protection. I feel just as great when sailing on HME2 as on HME1,

樣好，只要我們達成我們的目標。

我曾經在野外步行到極高處去鳥瞰周圍景觀或地理，或在家研究太空衛星影像享受這種高度視角。如今，我可以從無人機鏡頭的高角度觀察。這就是當探險家的極端，無論舒不舒適，傳統或前衛。我可以探險，用我的風格探險。除非不得已，我肯定偏好後者。

傳統上，探險家在西方很受尊崇，有皇室、政府和學術機構贊助。在東方，不知何故，許多人認為這種非常專業但非傳統的職業平凡又多餘，或根本就是浪費時間跟金錢。如果探險活動是由跟他們一樣的亞洲人主導的話，他們更是如此覺得。

當我為美國的國家地理雜誌探索，搭頭等艙住五星級飯店，比起我自己創立帶領，設在香港的 CERS，加諸在身上的光環與尊重似乎比較多。儘管如此，我們被 CNN 專題報導過十三次，許多故事登上世界知名媒體，包括探索頻道，這些應該能為我們的奢侈帶來辯護，證實我們開創性的努力，無論是探索或是保育工作的努力。這一直是我的慰藉，或許對我身邊勤奮不懈的夥伴也如是。

Drone view of Tropic of Cancer / 無人機拍攝的北回歸線景觀

as long as our purpose is fulfilled.

I have hiked to great heights and altitudes to have a bird's eye view of the landscape or geography around me in the field, or enjoyed such high perspectives at home by studying satellite images from space. These days, I may observe from such a high angle through the camera of a drone above head. Such are the extremes of being an explorer, in comfort or discomfort, traditional or Avant-garde. I can explore, or explore with style. Unless I must, I certainly prefer the latter.

Traditionally, explorers were revered in the West, patronized by royalty, gov-

幸好，亞洲對探險的鄙視可能正在改變，越來越多年輕人接觸到全世界其他地方，我們的宇宙和價值觀逐漸趨同。現在，我們有許多支持和贊助資金直接來自個人，他們看出我們努力拓展人類知識邊疆的同時也嘗試保存我們的發現事物。

當我們把 *HM Explorer* 停泊在欽敦江岸正好在北緯 23.5°處，我們在地理上所謂的北回歸線，我就在想這些。現在這條線或許並不出名，但對我們夏至中午站在這裡的許多人來說它仍然很重要，這時太陽會在頭頂正上方，地上不會照出影子。

Monk U Pan Nate Sa / 僧侶烏潘內薩

ernments, and scholarly institutions. In the East, somehow, many people look at such a highly-skilled yet unconventional profession as mundane and super-fluous, or a downright waste of time and money. It is even more so if explora-tion is conducted by one of their own kind, an Asian.

There seemed to be much more aura and respect accorded to me when I ex-plored for the US-based National Geographic, flying First Class and staying at Five-star hotels, than when I founded and headed CERS, an outfit based in Hong Kong. Nonetheless, our recognition in thirteen features by CNN and multiple stories in leading world media, including the Discovery Channel, should have vindicated our extravagance, and validated our pioneering en-deavors, be it in exploration or in our efforts in conservation. That is one last-ing consolation to me, as well as perhaps to those who have worked tirelessly along my side.

Fortunately, disdain for exploration may be changing in Asia, as more and more of our young people are exposed to the rest of the world, and our universe and values become more homogenized. Today, much of our support and fund-ing comes directly from private individuals who see the value of our efforts in expanding mankind's knowledge over the next horizon while attempting to preserve what we have discovered.

These were my thoughts when we docked our HM Explorer along the bank of

三年前我們用 GPS 標籤標記了這個地點，在附近只有
一個僧侶的 Phar Tin 寺，我們捐獻建造了一座小白塔。
它將成為留給未來世代的地標，讓他們在跨越緬甸這條
最重要的河流時，清楚知道這個地點。

今天，我們又遇到那個僧侶。烏潘內薩（U Pan Nate
Sa）今年 74 歲，在 28 年前出家。我決定在對岸捐另一
座塔，跟第一座相同，以標出這條線。我走下河岸在一
棵樹上塗漆記錄我想建塔的地方。「把樹砍掉蓋在這個
位置上，」我說。我還來不及繼續指示，我們的緬甸經

Chefs preparing BBQ / 廚師們準備烤肉

the Chindwin River exactly at 23.5° North latitude, a line we call the Tropic
of Cancer geographically. Such a line may not be very well known today, but
it remains crucial for many of us who would stand here during mid-day of the
summer solstice, when the sun is directly overhead, casting no shadow of our-
selves on the ground.

Three years ago we marked the position of this spot with a GPS marker, and,
at nearby Phar Tin monastery with one lone monk, we commissioned a small
white pagoda to be constructed. This has become a landmark for future gener-
ations, such that they would know the spot as they cross the line on one of the
most important rivers of Myanmar.

Today, we met that monk again. U Pan Nate Sa is 74 years old and had joined
monkhood 28 years ago. I had decided to commission another pagoda, twin
to the first one, across the river to mark the line. I stepped off the river bank
to paint and mark a tree where I wanted to erect the pagoda. "Cut the tree
and put the pagoda where it is standing," I said. Sandra, our Myanmar Man-
ager, quickly stopped me before I could give further instructions. "You must
not say such thing in front of a tree. It can hear and would feel distressed,"
Sandra reprimanded me. "Ok, ok, please ask him to move over a bit to make
space for an important landmark, both religious and geographic," I managed
to be as diplomatic as possible. I was feeling very pleased that we have now
on the same trip contributed to both Buddhism and Christianity, a balanced

理珊卓連忙阻止我。「不能在樹的面前說這種話。它聽得見會覺得沮喪，」珊卓斥責我。「好吧，好吧，請它讓開一點騰出空間給宗教和地理上的重要地標，」我盡力使用外交辭令。我很高興我們這趟旅行對佛教和基督教都有貢獻，這種平衡法很符合 CERS 的風格。

不過狗屎運在河邊小鎮再度降臨。沿河岸步道散步時，我看到一家小首飾店。玻璃展示小櫃裡面有幾件完成品。有四件銀戒指，其中一件上面刻了字母。正是「HM」。「為什麼刻上 HM ？」我問製作所有商品的年輕老闆。「我想總有人會喜歡，」他回答。真是恰當，二十四歲的珠寶匠 Zaw Zaw 也可以去當個算命師，他將戒指秤重計價。不久，戒指就進了我的口袋。

作為這趟河流旅途的終章，我們認真的廚師在岸上準備了美妙的烤肉餐，同時我們團隊在緬甸第一座標出北回歸線的佛塔邊準備享受豪華野餐。兩位大班在長桌兩端就座。約翰‧史崔克蘭是匯豐銀行的大班，而我仍是探險的大班！適當的奢侈？管他的！

approach synonymous with our CERS style.

But serendipity hit again at a river town. Strolling the promenade along the river, I saw a tiny jewelry shop. Behind its small boxed display glass case were a few finished items. There were four silver rings, one had alphabets inscriped on it. "HM" it reads. "Why HM?" I asked of the young owner who crafted all the pieces. "I thought someone would like it," came his answer. How appropriate, Zaw Zaw the 24-years jeweler who could also weigh in as a fortune-teller weighed the ring to price it. Before long, it was in my pocket.

As a finale to our river journey, our dedicated chefs cooked up a wonderful meal of barbeque on the bank while our team prepared to enjoy a sumptuous picnic lunch next to our first pagoda marking the Tropic of Cancer in Myanmar. At the two ends of the table, two Taipans took their seats. John Strickland was Taipan of HSBC, and I still remain the Taipan of Exploration! Measured Decadence? So be it!

Gold pagoda on Chindwin at high flood / 欽敦江淹水時的黃金佛塔

FIRST HOUSEHOLD AT THE IRRAWADDY SOURCE

Quwa Village, Zayu Tibet – October 2, 2017

伊洛瓦底江源頭第一家

伊洛瓦底江源頭第一家

游牧人最後一季

營地上的矮灌木正在變換色彩，變成黃色，橘色，深紅色。我們的海拔位於 3900 米高。初秋的霜降在 4000 米高的地方，這裡的葉子開始換上新的色彩。營地不遠處是氂牛跟犏牛（氂牛與家畜牛的混種）的高地放牧草原。

Tseren Sangmo 和她的阿姨 Yishi Lacho 是這高地草原上唯二的兩個人。大約七年前她們蓋的這座木屋成為伊洛瓦底江源頭上的第一戶人家。每年她們會在這裡待上兩個月，從八月到十月初。再過五天她們的家族裡就會有三位男性過來，幫忙她們撤營回家，從圖拉村的家走到這裡必須花上四天的功夫。

過去兩個月，六月跟七月，Sangmo 和 Lacho 在更高地方的放牧，再往上海拔兩百米的地方。在那邊她們住的木屋也是像這裡的。回到圖拉村可以放牧的草原很少，所以只有留在冬天才用再放牧。夏天他們將家畜趕到曲瓦

FIRST HOUSEHOLD AT THE IRRAWADDY SOURCE

Last season of a nomad camp

The low shrub above our basecamp is changing a coat of colors, into yellow, orange, and crimson red. We are at 3900 meters. It indicates that frost has arrived at 4000 meters, thus the foliage change. Not far from our camp is the high pasture for the Tibetan yak and zho (a hybrid between yak and cow) grazing ground.

Tseren Sangmo and her aunt Yishi Lacho are the only souls at this high pasture. The log shed they built some seven years ago can be considered the first household at the Irrawaddy source. Here they would spend two months of the year, from August to early October. In another five days, their family members, perhaps three men, would arrive from home, four days march away, to help them decamp to go home.

For the previous two months, June and July, Sangmo and Lacho were at a higher camp, another 200 meters higher, at another grazing ground. There, they live in a shed similar to this one. Back home in the village of Gula, pasture is scarce and thus kept only for winter grazing. They herd their

村旁可以付費放牧的草原。一頭家畜，一季收費人民幣30元。三十多頭來自三個家庭的家畜，總共要付一千多人民幣。

但是現在的光景大大不如前幾個世代那樣美好，甚至不能跟十年前相較。今年是 Sangmo 跟 Lacho 最後一次來這裡放牧。Lacho 告訴我，他的家人決定要把家畜們都賣掉，然後她要找其他的工作。去鎮裡或城市裡工作的收入會比較好也比較輕鬆。Sangmo 不確定她一個人可不可以應付剩下的家畜，明年可能也不會回來放

Sangmo eating her meal / Sangmo 正在吃飯

livestock here to the adjacent Quwa village and paid a fee to use their pasture for summer grazing. For each animal, they would pay 30 Yuan for seasonal usage. Herding over 30 animals belonging to three families from their home, they would pay upward of a thousand Yuan.

But things are not as rosy as generations ago, or even just ten years ago. This will be the last season for Sangmo and Lacho to herd their animals here. Lacho told me that her family would soon sell all their animals while she would look for other work. Going to work in towns or cities promise better pay, and easier work. Xangmo is not sure whether she alone could handle the

Lacho in front of shed / Lacho 於木屋前

牧了。

「你不會想念這地方嗎？」我問 Lacho。「當然會，雖然這工作真的很辛苦。」Lacho 回應。不管是下雨，放晴還是下冰雹，他們一整天都要工作。「我想我只會留下個兩頭牛在家，把其他的都賣掉，」她又說，「每一頭我都叫得出名字，每頭我都知道。」她蹲下擠牛奶時微笑地說。「我們是最後剩下的三戶人家了，至今還養著家畜的！」Lacho 的口吻瞬間轉成了淡淡的哀傷。

這工作越來越難持續下去。十九頭犛牛跟乳牛一年所產的奶，用手動機器攪動大概可以做成一百公斤的犛牛奶油。做完奶油剩下的乳水曬乾後做成奶渣。這兩樣東西大部分都是他們自己吃，奶渣混著粥就是他們的主食。其中大概幾十公斤的犛牛奶油會賣給朋友和鄰居。

每年當這兩位女士來高原放牧的時候，也正是冬蟲夏草的採收旺季。Lacho 比較有經驗，可以採到 350 根，一根值人民幣 35 元。Sangmo 還是新手，只能採到大約一百多根。

千年的傳統即將走入歷史。光光靠著豢養家畜已經不足以維生了，這種生存模式將被新的工作和生意所取

remaining livestock and would unlikely return to the herding ground next year.

"Won't you miss this place?" I asked of Lacho. "Yes, I would, though work is really hard," answered Lacho. Be it rain, shine or hail, they'll be working all day long. "I think I would only keep a couple of our animals at home, while the rest would be sold," she added. "I knew each animal by name and by heart," she said with a slight smile of intimacy as she squatted low while milking her cow. "We are already the last three families to keep to our livestock," Lacho spoke with a soft tone of sadness.

It seems less and less equitable as the years go by. The nineteen yaks and cows they own yields enough milk for one season which are churned by a hand-crank machine into maybe a hundred kilos of yak butter. The residual milky water is dried and made into a hard yogurt. Both are mainly for their own consumption, with the hard yogurt mixed into congee as part of their staple. Perhaps a few dozen kilos of yak butter would be sold to friends and neighbors.

As in past years, when the two ladies arrived at the high pasture, it would be also cordyceps collecting high season. Lacho is more experienced in looking for such high-country fungus and took in about 350 pieces, each worth Rmb 35 Yuan. Sangmo is new to this and only managed slightly over 100 pieces.

A thousand-year-old tradition is coming to a close. Livestock raising is no

Drying residual / 將乳水曬乾

代，為了有更好的收入。現在的環境和便利的運輸讓
藏人傳統的游牧文化與放牧生活沒辦法繼續，畜牧與
農業已不再時興。

Sangmo 今年 18 歲，她的阿姨 30 歲並有兩個小孩。
Sangmo 和 Lacho 都是龍年出生的，吉祥的年。「妳結婚
了嗎？有小孩嗎？」我問 Sangmo，她長得很漂亮，身
高超過 180 公分。「沒有，我沒交過男朋友，連戀愛也
沒談過……」她這樣回答。

「像妳這麼漂亮一定有很多的追求者。」我繼續追問。
「我家裡不允許我自己選擇對象，我的父母會幫我安排

longer even enough for subsistence, replaced by newer and more lucrative work and business opportunities. The new condition and transportation convenience have made much of the Tibetan traditional lifestyle obsolete. Nomadic culture, even pastoral tradition, that of tending to both livestock and agriculture, are no longer in style.

Sangmo is 18 years of age. Her aunt is twelve years older at 30, with two children. Both Sangmo and Lacho were born in the Year of the Dragon, an auspicious sign. "Are you married and have kids?" I asked of Sangmo, seeing that she is very beautiful and standing tall at over 1.8 meters. "No, I've never even had a boyfriend or ever been in love," came her reply.

"But you are so beautiful you must have many suitors," I pursued further. "At my family, I cannot choose to get marry by my own free will. My parents would arrange whom I should marry," said Sangmo while looking down with shyness. Her Chinese is totally fluent, thanks to six years attending a local school before she started herding animals at age 15. As for Lacho, she and her elder sister are both betrothed to the same man. Each has produced two kids for the husband.

Through Sangmo and Lacho, I found out that practically all marriages at their village are arranged by parents. In that sense, their livestock seems to have a more liberal and free life than their masters, being able to choose their own mate. When it would be Sangmo's turn to get married, the five hybrid

結婚的對象，」Sangmo 低下頭來顯得有些害羞。她的中文很流利，這都歸功於她在 15 歲開始放牧之前曾經在當地學校念了六年的書。而 Lacho 和她的姊姊則是許配給同一個男人。姊妹跟同個先生各生了兩個小孩。

透過 Sangmo 和 Lacho 我才知道原來這村子裡所有的婚姻都是由父母安排的。這些家畜顯然要比牠們的主人自由多了，至少可以自由選擇跟誰在一起和交配。等到 Sangmo 要出嫁的時候，這五隻跟犛牛混種的犏牛就是她的嫁妝。

我邀請 Sangmo 和 Lacho 到我們的營地吃晚飯，但是她們回絕說工作還沒做完。對我們來說，她們非常的特別，她們是離伊洛瓦底江源頭最近的一戶人家。這條江流過 2200 公里才出海，沿著這條江住著成千上萬的人家。

真的是伊洛瓦底江源頭的第一家庭，只是她們沒有空軍一號可搭。當她們結束最後這趟游牧並啟程回家時，她們將會騎在馬背上，趕著犛牛和乳牛，呼吸著山上新鮮的空氣，這種我們城市人從來沒有呼吸過的空氣。

Sangmo carrying water / Sangmo 揹水

yaks belonging to the family would become her dowry, going with her to her husband's home.

I invited Sangmo and Lacho to visit our camp and join us for dinner. But they declined, citing that their day's work would take up all their time. For us, the two are very special, the first household closest to the Irrawaddy River source. Downriver there are thousands and tens of thousands of families living along this great river which flows for over 2200 kilometers until it reaches the sea.

Yes, this is literally the First Family at the Irrawaddy source. No, they don't have an Air Force One to travel in. But as they begin their last journey home from this grazing ground, they would be on their horses, driving with them their yak and cow herd, breathing the fresh mountain air that many of us in the city has never even know to exist.

RETURN TO THE SOURCE OF THE IRRAWADDY

Irrawaddy Source, Zayu, Tibet – October 3, 2017

回到伊洛瓦底江源頭

回到伊洛瓦底江源頭〈續集〉再加 1.4 公里

座標：北緯 *28.7340°* 東經 *97.8725°E*

(28°44'04"N 97°52'35"E)

海拔高度：*4,821* 公尺 *(15,909 feet)*

時間：*10* 點 *38* 分　日期：*2017* 年 *10* 月 *03* 日

我的手凍僵了，連相機都不聽使喚，按下快門後相機會停頓好幾秒才開始運作。然後就當機，需要重新開機。風呼呼地吹著，這裡的氣溫肯定是低於零度因為雨水都變成了冰雹。一定是海拔的關係，海拔 4821 公尺。要不然就是河神，此刻我與團隊抵達伊洛瓦底江的源頭與分水嶺。

「就是這裡了」我下了指令，在兩條小溪匯合處做了記號。再過去就是沼澤和水堀，這裡就是源頭。我的 *iPad* 整個早上都開著，特殊的 *app* 追蹤我們的行徑、時間、距離，還有一些從營地出發的關鍵數據。

RETURN TO THE SOURCE OF THE IRRAWADDY (PART II)

Just for 1.4 kilometers of additional length

Coordinates: 28.7340°N 97.8725°E (28°44'04"N 97°52'35"E)

Altitude: 4,821 meters (15,909 feet) Time: 10:38 Date: 2017-10-03

My hands are frozen and numb. My camera has gone wild, taking photos in delayed mode a few seconds after I push the shutter. Then it momentarily dies and I have to reboot it. The wind is blowing and the temperature must be below zero as rain turns to hail. It must be the altitude, 4821 meters in elevation. Otherwise it has to be the river god, as my team and I reach the watershed and source of the Irrawaddy River.

"This is it," I gave out the order, marking a small drop-off where two tiny streams trickle downward joining each other. Beyond and above are marshes with water holes, merging to become the source stream. My iPad has been on all morning, with my special App tracking our route, time, distance and several other crucial data from our basecamp to here.

Lungda at source / 源頭上的風馬旗

"Let's mark the spot with the prayer flag," I give out another order to my team. Soon three poles are stuck in the ground and a string of colorful flags span the source of the Irrawaddy. My next move is almost like clockwork, something I had dreamed of, as well as performed, several times before, each time when I reached the source of a great river; the Yangtze, Mekong, Yellow River, or Salween. I kneel down striding the creek, and with my two hands I bring the water to my mouth. Drinking from the source is always a very sacred moment, especially for an explorer.

I make several screen-shots on my iPad satellite image to record the necessary data, most importantly, the coordinates of this spot – 28°44'04"N 97°52'35"E. Time of arrival is of course noted. My Omega says 10:38. It's been almost three hours of continuous riding on horseback since we left basecamp at 7:48 this morning. Next my team passes me three Aluminum water bottles which I use to collect the source water for later analysis back home. Our caravan helpers are watching with amazement. Why do these people make such a big deal about a tiny stream?

Despite high wind at the watershed pass, Xavier launches the drone and takes an aerial view of the source just as each of us lets off into thin air a stack of Lungda, or paper Wind Horse, which are sacred offerings to the gods. As the Wind Horse take to flight, our horses on the ground got into

Data & routing to sourcen / 到源頭的數據資料與路徑

「就是這裡，用瑪尼旗做記號，」我給團隊下達另一個命令。很快地三根桿子立在地上，一串色彩鮮豔的瑪尼旗飄在依洛瓦底江的源頭上。接下來我的動作就像到長江、湄公河、黃河、瀾滄江的源頭一樣。我跪在源頭前，兩手捧起水就我的口。飲下源頭水一直都是很神聖的一刻，尤其是對一位探險家來說。

好幾張 *iPad* 上的衛星影像都被我截圖下來成為重要的數據，最重要的是這個點的經緯度：北緯 *28°44'04"* 東經 *97°52'35"*。抵達時間當然也被記錄下來，我的歐米茄手錶顯示 *10* 點 *38* 分。今天早上 *7* 點 *48* 分我們從營地出發，在馬背上騎了近三個鐘頭。接著，我的團隊遞給我 *3* 瓶鋁製水壺讓我收集源頭水帶回去做分析。我

frenzy and almost went into a stampede, stirred on by the drone. Fortunately our caravan helpers quickly held them down as commotion gradually subsided. Several members of the team are searching the ground, looking for special rocks as memorabilia to take home. I get a bit greedy and take in a few more sip of the source water, until my hands are too numb to continue.

Before we turn to mount our horses on the return journey, we take out the CERS flag and make our group photo, all nine of us from the CERS team. Everyone has a smile of contentment on his or her face. I, too, feel another mission accomplished. The fifth river source that I have had the good fortune to reach and define; not a small geographic feat.

The less than six hours roundtrip on horseback from basecamp to the source, covering 15.5 kilometers, seems little compared to my first journey to the Yangtze source in 1985. That roundtrip took me nine days on horseback. But the Irrawaddy source is no less important in my mind. It's like having five children, each important and unique in his or her own way.

It may seem obsessive to return to the river source of a great river of Asia within slightly over four short months. But in the past, I have returned to the Yangtze source three times, 1985, 1995 and 2005, just to verify and correct our own work results. For the Irrawaddy, it had to be done, the sooner the better, given my gradually waning energy. High elevation work

們馬隊的幫手們在一旁驚訝的看著。這群人為什麼對這
一條小溪看得這麼重要？

儘管分水嶺隘口的風很大，李伯達還是將空拍機升空，
從空中捕捉我們揮撒風馬旗的景象，風馬是獻給神明
的。當風馬飄向天空時，地上的馬兒卻因為空拍機而受
了驚嚇，差一點踩踏傷人，還好我們馬隊的幫手及時控

is not compatible with someone soon to reach seven decades in life. But for
now, I still have a bit of mileage remaining.

Upon returning from the Irrawaddy source in late May, our long-time friend
Martin Ruzek, formerly a NASA scientist, revealed to me that beyond
the source lake, Jingla Co, there was a feeder stream under the snow that
stretched another 1.4 kilometers further up the watershed. When the snow

Team marching pass Jingla Co / 隊伍騎經金格拉湖

制住牠們。團隊裡好幾位成員在地上尋找特別的石頭要帶回家當作紀念品。而我則是有一點貪心，多喝了幾口源頭水，直到我的手指都凍僵了。

準備騎馬返回前，我們拿出 CERS 的旗子拍團體照，這次 CERS 總共有九個人成功抵達源頭。每個人臉上都露出滿足的笑容。而我，覺得又達成一個任務。很幸運地我來到第五條河流的源頭，定位這個源頭；這在地理學上可不是件小事。

從營地到源頭騎馬往返約 15.5 公里，差不多六個鐘頭；但跟我在 1985 年去長江探源的旅程相較就小巫見大巫了。長江那趟我騎了九天的馬。伊洛瓦底江探源的經驗也不差。好像生五個小孩一樣，每個都很重要，每個也很特別。

才過了四個多月就再回到亞洲最偉大河流之一的源頭好像有點過分了。1985 年，1995 年，2005 年我回去過長江的源頭三次，只為了確定跟校正我們的發現是否正確。對伊洛瓦底江也是，得趁我還有體力的時候。在高海拔工作對一位快要七十歲的人來說確實有些吃力。但是現在，我還有體力。

melted during the summer, satellite images would show clearly this feeder stream. We must return to mark this definitive source of the Irrawaddy.

From our Zhongdian Center we headed for Zayu County in southeastern Tibet. Along the way, three rockslides, products of tail end of the raining season, deterred our progress. One took six hours to clear, the other two, one half day and a full day. Other unexpected deterrents were the result of recent border tension between India and China, making security check points more frequent and thorough. This wasn't the case back in May. The upcoming 19th Party Congress added another layer of security as government and police do not want to see any disruptive incidents during that time.

Due to such measures, negotiating for horses took longer than usual as the villagers needed to get permission from above to rent us their horses. We needed a total of 15 horses and six caravan helpers. True to form of the old commune tradition of fairness, the villagers made a draw on whose horses would get rented, as well as which individual would become a helper. During the day and a half in waiting, I had the opportunity to visit and interview the first herding family tending to their livestock near our basecamp; literally the first family at the source of the Irrawaddy.

The river we followed to Jingla Co (the source lake) and onwards to the 1.4 kilometer feeder stream source is called Jiutong (or Dutong depending

五月底從伊洛瓦底江源頭回來時，我的老友 Martin
Ruzek 跟我說在金格拉源頭湖的上面，離分水嶺 1.4 公
里遠的地方還有條小溪藏在雪底下，老友 Martin 曾經
是 NASA 的科學家。當夏天來了，雪也融了之後，衛星
圖會變得比較清楚，可以看見這條小溪。那時就說好，
我們一定要回去，再次確定伊洛瓦底江的源頭。

從中甸中心出發前往西藏東南部的察隅縣，途中受到雨
季過後的三個不同地方的大落石滑坡而阻礙了前進。光
是清除其中一塊滑坡就花了六個鐘頭，另外兩塊各花了
半天跟一整天。還有預期外的阻力來自中國與印度邊界
上的緊張情勢，檢查站變多了，檢查的也更徹底，五月
的時候情況並非如此。即將展開的十九大會議也是讓安
檢升級的因素之一，因為政府與警察都不希望這段期間
有任何意外發生。

因為上述的原因，要跟村民租馬匹就變得困難多了。
村民必需跟上級取得許可後才可以把馬匹租給我們。
我們總共需要 15 匹馬和 6 位馬隊助手。為了公平起見，
村民們用抽籤的方式決定出租誰的馬還有誰會當助手。
一天半的等待時間，剛好給了我一個機會去探訪在營
地附近放牧的第一戶人家，真的是在伊洛瓦底江源頭

Cars in scale / 車子的比例大小

on pronunciation). Two ridges away is another stream, the Yepo, which is only 40 meters shorter in length from its source to its confluence with the Jiutong. This created a dilemma in my mind.

For a river as great as the Irrawaddy, which flows for over 2200 kilometers before reaching the sea, what is 40 meters in difference? Let alone that the two sources are so very close to each other. This seems a perfect case to make a call that the Irrawaddy River has a twin source, no different from two twin

的第一戶人家。

我們隨著 *Jiutong* 河〈或稱 *Dutong*〉來到金格拉湖〈源頭湖〉再前行 1.4 公里來到源頭。兩個山嶺外還有另一條溪 *Yepo*，從源頭到它與 *Jiutong* 河的匯流處，長度則少了 40 公尺。這讓我陷入兩難。

伊洛瓦底江如此偉大的一條河流，流經 2200 公里才出海，區區 40 公尺的差異又算什麼？而且兩個源頭又是這麼接近彼此。給予伊洛瓦底江兩個源頭似乎是合適的，就像一對雙胞胎，長的都一樣，只是一位頭髮多一點而已。

世界上充滿了爭論，人與人之間，或是國與國之間，爭取誰最偉大、最強大、最有力。偉大與力量同時也應該伴隨著更多的責任與義務。我們彼此可以和平地住在一起，各自都可以為這偉大的世界做出貢獻。*Jiutong* 河與 *Yepo* 河這兩個雙胞胎就是最完美的比喻，它們與上百條上千條的河流一起成為偉大的伊洛瓦底江。

siblings, one having a bit more hair than the other.

The world is full of contention among people or countries wanting to be the greatest, strongest and most powerful. With greatness and power, there should also come more responsibilities and obligations. But we can also live alongside each other peacefully, each serving its purpose towards a greater world. The two twin streams of Jiutong and Yepo are a perfect metaphor; together with hundreds and thousands of streams, they make up the great Irrawaddy River.

Group at Source / 源頭的團體照

國家圖書館出版品預行編目 (CIP) 資料

自然所想 / 黃效文著.
-- 初版 . -- [新北市]：依揚想亮人文 , 2017.12
面； 公分
ISBN 978-986-93841-6-2（平裝）
1. 遊記 2. 世界地理

719   106023922

自
然
所
想

作者・黃效文 ｜ 發行人・劉鋆 ｜ 責任編輯・王思晴 ｜ 美術編輯・Rene Lo ｜ 翻譯
李建興・依揚想亮人文事業有限公司 ｜ 法律顧問・達文西個資暨高科技法律事務所 ｜
出版社・依揚想亮人文事業有限公司 ｜ 經銷商・聯合發行股份有限公司 ｜ 地址・新
北市新店區寶橋路 235 巷 6 弄 6 號 2 樓 ｜ 電話・02 2917 8022 ｜ 印刷・禹利電子分
色有限公司 ｜ 初版一刷・2017 年 12 月（平裝） ｜ ISBN・000-000-00000-0-0 ｜ 定價
400 元 ｜ 版權所有 翻印必究 ｜ Print in Taiwan

依揚想亮 出版書目